AN EARLY

VICTORIAN

ALBUM

AN EARLY VICTORIAN ALBUM

The photographic masterpieces (1843–1847)

of David Octavius Hill and Robert Adamson,

edited and introduced by Colin Ford,

and with an interpretive essay by Roy Strong

Alfred A. Knopf, New York

19  76

THIS IS A BORZOI BOOK
PUBLISHED BY ALFRED A. KNOPF, INC.

Both authors are grateful to Robin Hutchison and his staff
at the Scottish National Portrait Gallery for their help. Dr. Strong
wishes to thank Mrs. Doris Langley-Moore for her advice over
costume in the photographs and Mr. Ford thanks Dr. William C.
Sturtevant, of the Department of Anthropology in the National Museum of
Natural History, Smithsonian Institution, and all those correspondents, too
numerous to mention, who have filled gaps in his knowledge. It has been
particularly exciting to make contact with so many direct descendants of those who sat for
calotypes and from them has come much of the new information published in this book.
The authors' debt to previous writers on Hill and Adamson is acknowledged in the text.

Library of Congress Cataloging in Publication Data
Hill, David Octavius, 1802–1870.   An early Victorian Album.
London ed. (J. Cape) has subtitle: the Hill/Adamson collection.
Includes bibliographical references and index.
1. Hill, David Octavius, 1802–1870. 2. Adamson, Robert, 1821–1848.
3. Photography, Artistic. 4. Photography—Portraits. 5. Calotype.
I. Adamson, Robert, 1821–1848. II. Ford, Colin John, (date) III. Title.
TR651.H53 1974b   779'.092'4   74-21315
ISBN 0-394-49733-3

Manufactured in the United States of America
First American Edition

For Julia/Margaret

Contents

AN EARLY

VICTORIAN

ALBUM

INTRODUCTION

COLIN FORD

NEGATIVES AND POSITIVES:

PHOTOGRAPHY FROM NIÉPCE TO

ADAMSON

In 1951 an Arts Council exhibition, "Masterpieces of Victorian Photography 1840–1900," was arranged at London's Victoria and Albert Museum by the eminent photographic historian Helmut Gernsheim. It aroused great interest in an art form which had hardly ever before been given serious attention, and Victorian photographs seem ever since to have been steadily growing both in popularity and salesroom value. The growth is not entirely due to fashion or shrewd investment: it is also an overdue recognition of the fact that photography in the nineteenth century truly flowered in Britain, though it had actually been invented in France.

Queen Victoria herself, who had come to the throne less than two years before the discovery of practical methods of photography was announced, gave the new art considerable encouragement. She often wore a signet ring in which were set tiny photographic portraits of five close members of her family, and she and Prince Albert had their own darkroom at Windsor Castle, fitted out in the first months of 1854 with the help of the famous photographer Roger Fenton. Albert's Great Exhibition of 1851 (of which Gernsheim's "Masterpieces" was in part a centenary celebration) was dedicated to the triumphs of British technology; it was therefore natural that it should use and display thousands of photographs. "Honourable mention" in the photography on paper section was made of the portraits taken by two Scotsmen who had stopped work four years earlier—David Octavius Hill (1802–70) and Robert Adamson (1821–48)—and there is good reason to believe that the first example of the new medium ever seen by Prince Albert was a Hill and Adamson calotype of Elizabeth Rigby Eastlake (1809–93). She had married

---

Charles Eastlake (later Sir Charles) in 1849, and, as he was not only President of the Royal Academy of Arts and Director of the National Gallery but also the first President of the London Photographic Society, founded in 1853 (and soon, favoured with the patronage of Queen Victoria and Prince Albert, allowed to style itself "Royal"), she moved in the most influential art and social circles in Britain. In a letter to a friend in Edinburgh dated July 27th, 1891, Lady Eastlake wrote: "A Talbotype of me, full-length, in a white silk dress, eyes down, was the first specimen of the photographic art that the Prince Consort saw, and excited his curiosity."* It seems likely that this is the picture reproduced in figure 1; the description certainly fits.

1. Miss Elizabeth Rigby—page 119.

Six years after the Great Exhibition, Lady Eastlake wrote an article on photography in which she spoke of her admiration for Hill and Adamson:

> Photography made but slow way in England; and the first knowledge even of her existence came back to this country from across the Border. It was in Edinburgh, where the first earnest, professional practice of the art began, and the calotypes of Messrs. Hill and Adamson remain to this day the most picturesque specimens of the new discovery.†

"Talbotype" and "calotype" are alternative names for the same photographic process, and most critics today would still accord those taken by Hill and Adamson supremacy among the earliest works of photography. This book, *An Early Victorian Album*, with its two hundred fifty-five reproductions of their best calotypes, is certainly dedicated to that proposition.

The National Portrait Gallery Albums

The pictures in this book do not in fact come from one album, but from three. These form a presentation set of *Calotype Studies by D. O. Hill, R. S. A. and Robert Adamson*, dated on the spines "Edinburgh,

*Quoted in Andrew Elliott, *Calotypes by D. O. Hill and R. Adamson*. Both Elliott and his son George, who took over the book from him, died before work on it could be completed. Thirty-eight copies were made up from the surviving sheets by another son, Dr. Andrew Elliott, and published in Edinburgh for private circulation in 1928. Copy No. 14 is in the National Portrait Gallery, London.

†*The Quarterly Review*, No. 101, London, March 1857. (Published anonymously, as was the magazine's practice, but certainly written by Lady Eastlake in the winter of 1856–57.)

1848–1848," and presented to the Royal Academy of Arts in London soon after Adamson's untimely death at the age of twenty-seven. Hill actually proposed the gift in 1846, and the dedication bears that date: "To the President and Members of the Royal Academy of Fine Arts, London. These attempts to apply artistically the recently discovered process of The Calotype, Are, with great respect, Inscribed and presented by their Obedient Humble Servant, D. O. Hill. Edinburgh, 26 July, 1846."

This implies that Hill was making an effort to have his part in the taking of the calotypes accepted in the London art world as being of artistic importance, though the albums may also partly have been a fraternal gift from the Royal Scottish Academy, of which Hill was secretary, to its English counterpart. In any case, the Royal Academy duly acknowledged the gift,* put the three albums into its library (they are recorded in its catalogue of 1874), and left them there, virtually unopened, until 1967. Once having rediscovered them, the Academy made unsuccessful attempts to publish the albums, and then, in 1972, decided to sell them in order to raise funds to build a public display gallery for Michelangelo's priceless tondo of *The Madonna and Child with the Infant Saint John,* which had hitherto been hidden away in one of the private rooms of Burlington House.

The National Portrait Gallery in London had started a Department of Film and Photography, separate from its other activities, earlier in 1972 (it had actually been systematically collecting photographic portraits since 1917). Like the other national institutions with interests in photography, it knew nothing of the impending sale until the first story appeared in a London evening newspaper, for the intended auctioneers, Sotheby's, had released the news before mailing catalogues of the sale. This was scheduled for December 13th, giving the Director and staff of the Gallery precious little time to stop an event which they, like most people interested in the possibility of building up a proper national and public collection of historic photographs in Britain, considered potentially disastrous.

By a fortunate coincidence, photographs over seventy years old and sold for more than £100 had just been made subject to export

---

* In a letter from its secretary, dated December 26th, 1849, addressed to Hill and still kept in the files of the Royal Scottish Academy: "Dear Sir, I laid your three volumes of Calotypes before the President and Council of the Royal Academy at our last meeting, and am directed to convey to you their warmest thanks for your liberal and interesting addition to our library—They were inspected with great interest and elicited the highest approbation.   I am, Dear Sir Your Obedt. Servant   John P. Knight."

licensing control (as works of art and historic manuscripts had been for many years). The Trustees of the National Portrait Gallery met and drafted a resolution urging the Royal Academy to withdraw the albums from the sale. This the Academy did, after a couple of days' energetic press support for the Gallery's stand, so as to give all interested parties time to consider what to do. These "interested parties" included curatorial staff from most of the other museums and galleries connected with photography, who had given the National Portrait Gallery considerable support in the campaign.

The press coverage did not stop. Radio, television, and particularly the Sunday papers attacked the original decision to sell and bemoaned the absence of a national photographic archive in Britain. Although the National Portrait Gallery made no claim to be setting up such an institution (its own archival aims being clearly limited to a very specialized area), the *Sunday Times*, the Gallery's most forthright ally at this stage, published an appeal to its readers to send their old photographs to the new Department of Film and Photography, and for weeks afterwards they arrived in sackfuls. Roy Strong, the Director of the National Portrait Gallery, wrote to the President of the Royal Academy: "Should they [the albums] be offered to the National Portrait Gallery, every effort would be made to raise funds for their acquisition . . . our concern is for saving the photographs for a national collection."

At last, almost exactly a month later, the Academy offered the albums to the Gallery for the sum of £32,178.50, making them the most expensive set of photographs in the world. Though this seemed an enormous price, it may well have been a bargain, since Sotheby's had revealed the presence of an American prepared to bid up to £70,000. But the Academy's offer posed one awful dilemma for the Gallery; the President and Council of the Academy had made the sale "conditional upon the National Portrait Gallery's producing this sum without a public appeal." Presumably they feared being attacked again in the same way as they had been in 1962, when they accepted appeal money for Leonardo's cartoon *Madonna and Child with Saint Anne and Saint John the Baptist*, but that they had at least offered to the nation before threatening to sell it at auction.

In any case, the Gallery did not have the money to buy the albums at this price, though its Trustees had pledged all the purchase money left in their kitty (a mere £3,000). This latest development in the story was also given wide press coverage, and an anonymous benefactor donated the entire sum to the Gallery. The albums were brought to the Gallery on January 26th, 1973, and, less than six weeks after this, an exhibition—which ran for five weeks and was seen by twenty-three thousand people—was opened and a paperback book* was published, containing reproductions of one-fourth of the photographs in the albums.

The National Portrait Gallery albums constitute perhaps the best-preserved large set of Hill and Adamson prints anywhere in the world, and it is right that they should be in a publicly owned collection in London. Though they, and the reproductions made from some of them, have already become familiar to a great number of people, it is desirable that reproductions of all the photographs in the complete albums should be made available in a more permanently accessible form—hence the present volume.

A significant part of the importance of Hill and Adamson derives from the fact, not always realized by some of those who joined in the fierce arguments over where the calotypes should find a home, that they were among the very earliest photographers in the world. They started work less than four years after the public announcement of photography, and Adamson was dead less than a decade after that announcement. As Helmut Gernsheim, whose name has already been invoked because of his influential role in the rediscovery of Victorian photography, says:

> Today David Octavius Hill and Robert Adamson are universally accorded first place in the annals of photography. The artistic spirit with which their photographs are imbued has impressed all succeeding generations, and it is indeed astonishing that in its very first years the new art should have reached its highest peak in the magnificent achievements of these two Scottish photographers.†

Niépce and Daguerre

In a way, photography *ought* to have been invented about 1800. The fact that silver nitrate is sensitive to light and darkens on exposure to it was discovered as early as 1727 by Johann Heinrich Schulze, and the *camera obscura*—which reflects images through a lens on

---

*Colin Ford, *The Hill/Adamson Albums: A Selection of Victorian Prints*, with an introduction by Roy Strong (Times Newspapers Ltd., London, 1973). I am most grateful to the publishers for permission to use material from that book in the following pages.
† Helmut and Alison Gernsheim, *The History of Photography* (Oxford University Press, London, 1955; revised and enlarged edition, Thames and Hudson, London, 1969).

to a sheet of paper or glass over which they can be traced—had been in existence for hundreds of years, being especially widely used throughout the eighteenth century. But these two elements of photography were never married. In 1802 Thomas Wedgwood, of the pottery family, recorded his experiments, begun two years earlier:

> A piece of paper, or other convenient material, was placed upon a frame and sponged over with a solution of nitrate of silver; it was then placed behind a painting on glass and the light traversing the painting produced a kind of copy upon the prepared paper, those parts in which the rays were least intercepted being of the darkest hues. Here, however, terminated the experiment; for although both Mr. Wedgwood and Sir Humphry Davy experimented carefully, for the purpose of endeavouring to fix the drawings thus obtained, yet the object could not be accomplished, and the whole ended in failure.*

Wedgwood and Davy are describing exactly how early photography began, and if they had known of Karl Wilhelm Scheele's discovery in 1777 that silver salts which have been exposed to light become insoluble when ammonia is poured on them, they would have had an acceptable fixative, and photography would have begun its history. Robert Adamson's first photographs, taken some forty years later, were in fact fixed with ammonia.

So the world's first photograph "from nature" was probably not taken until the summer of 1826—or it may even have been 1827. The precise date cannot be pinpointed with any certainty, but what is sure is that the photographer, and experimenter in the process since 1816 (he first described it in a letter to his brother, dated May 9th of that year), was Joseph Nicéphore Niépce (1765–1833). His first successful photograph was of rooftops and a barn, taken from the attic window of his home at St.-Loup-de-Varennes in central France. On the southern outskirts of the village today is a monumental slab of concrete, erected in 1933 to proclaim, as some historians (especially French ones) believe, that the invention of photography took place there in 1822. The justification for this date is that Niépce did manage to make a photographic copy of an engraving in that year, but

---

*Thomas Wedgwood and Humphry Davy, in the *Journal of the Royal Institution*, London, volume I, no. 9, 22 June 1802.

all the evidence indicates that his first true photograph "from nature" cannot have been taken for another four or five years.

Niépce called his process "heliography" (Greek *helios*, "sun"; *graphia*, "writing"), and, if the surviving picture* of his house is typical, it certainly needed a lot of help from the sun. From the shadows cast in both directions at once, it appears that an exposure of about eight hours was given (this is supported by another letter from Niépce to his brother), and even so the results are rather indistinct. He failed to arouse much interest in his invention, despite energetic efforts in France and England, where he addressed the Royal Society in 1827, and where George IV may have seen his pictures, since they were left at Windsor Castle for inspection.† It remained for another Frenchman, Louis Jacques Mandé Daguerre (1787–1851), to bring photography to practical application.

Daguerre had met Niépce soon after the latter had made his first photograph, and they entered into a contract of partnership in 1829. Daguerre's previous main preoccupation had been the diorama, and with his partner, the painter Charles Bouton, he operated these commercially and artistically successful shows both in Paris and in London (at 18 Park Square East, Regent's Park, where the building can still be seen). The diorama depended for its *trompe-l'œil* effect on huge (forty-five feet high by seventy feet wide), meticulously detailed panoramas painted on gauze screens to allow transformation scenes to be carried out by careful manipulation of light in front of and behind the gauze. To help him paint these, Daguerre made use of a *camera obscura*, and for years he tried to fix its images, spending days and nights in his laboratory on the premises of the Paris Diorama. Early in 1837 he succeeded in fixing images on sensitized silver-coated plates with a solution of common salt. Niépce had died four years earlier, and the new photographs, which had much better definition and shorter exposure times than Niépce's heliographs, became known as "daguerreotypes."

Daguerre, like Niépce, failed to find commercial backing for his discovery, but in 1839 he managed to sell it to the French government, which made it freely available in France, though Daguerre had shrewdly patented it in England just five days before signing his

---

* Now in the Gernsheim Collection, Humanities Research Center, the University of Texas at Austin.
† Letter from Niépce to his son Isidore, November 21st, 1827, now in the possession of Mme Henriette Niépce.

French government contract. Details of the process were announced publicly in Paris in August 1839 and in London in September. Daguerre, with a government salary from France and royalties from England, was on his way to becoming a rich man.

Photogenic Drawing

Niépce's photographs had been on pewter, Daguerre's on silvered copper. Such solid metal plates would not let light through them and were therefore unique pictures from which prints could not be made (though Niépce had conceived the idea of negative and positive images). Furthermore, being produced by a direct positive process, they made mirror-images, laterally transposed versions of reality, unless expensive prisms were used to correct them. For photography to advance, a negative-positive process had to be evolved, and here, at last, an English inventor made a decisive contribution to the story.

William Henry Fox Talbot (1800–77) was educated at Harrow School and Trinity College, Cambridge. He published his first scientific paper at age twenty-two and by 1833 had brought out twelve more, mainly on mathematical and optical subjects. In 1832 he became Liberal Member of Parliament for Chippenham, Wiltshire, and, while making the "Grand Tour" of Europe the following year, he used a *camera obscura*. Like Daguerre, he was soon fired with the notion of fixing its images:

> And this led me to reflect on the inimitable beauty of the pictures of nature's painting which the glass lens of the Camera throws upon the paper in its focus—fairy pictures, creations of a moment, and destined as rapidly to fade away. It was during these thoughts that the idea occurred to me . . . . . how charming it would be if it were possible to cause these natural images to imprint themselves durably, and remain fixed upon the paper. And why should it not be possible? I asked myself.*

Fox Talbot started experiments to make his dream reality as soon as he returned to England in 1834, and he took his first photograph "from nature"—like Niépce's, it was of his home, and it showed the diamond-latticed windows of Lacock Abbey in Wiltshire—in August 1835, with a tiny two-and-a-half-inch-square camera made by a local

---

* W. H. Fox Talbot, *The Pencil of Nature* (Longmans, London, 1844), the first published book to be illustrated with actual photographs.

carpenter. Christened a "mousetrap" by his wife, it used a chemically treated writing paper, and, as one can see from that first success, the second oldest photograph in existence (figure 2—now in the Science Museum, London), it took pictures only about an inch square. The surviving example is lilac, somewhat faded and out of focus and—most significantly—is what we would today recognize as a negative. The exposure it required was an hour or two, shorter than Niépce's eight hours, but much longer than Daguerre's twenty to thirty minutes.

2. The second oldest photograph in existence (Science Museum, London).

Fox Talbot was still involved in many other activities and experiments, publishing between 1834 and 1839 no less than eleven scientific papers on subjects quite unconnected with photography. During this time his only real progress with "photogenic drawing," as he called his invention, was to start making more than one positive from a negative by placing it on top of a second sheet of sensitized paper and exposing the latter to light through the negative.

The terms "negative" and "positive" were coined by Sir John Herschel (1792–1871), son of George III's private astronomer Sir William Herschel and a close friend of Fox Talbot's. He made some brief but brilliant forays into the subject and, within a week after the announcement of daguerreotypes, worked out his own completely independent kind of photography. He was the first to take successful photographs on glass (as in the later "collodion" process of Frederick Scott Archer, which was, in the 1850's, to oust all other processes, including those of Daguerre and Fox Talbot). Herschel's most important contribution was the discovery that "hypo" (sodium hyposulphate, or thiosulphate) was the best fixing agent because it efficiently washed away all the unaltered silver salts after the photograph had been processed. (His own surviving photogenic drawings are more faded than Fox Talbot's, perhaps because he did not realize the importance to permanence of washing away all the residual hypo before drying the photographs.) Herschel had discovered the existence of hypo twenty years earlier than his use of it as a fixative, but Fox Talbot, who must have had access to this information, used common salt and, later, potassium bromide or potassium iodide, none of which was as satisfactory a fixative as sodium thiosulphate.

Daguerre first publicly announced his invention (but without any details of how it worked) on January 7th, 1839, and within days Fox Talbot, who must have assumed that it involved a process very much like his own, was galvanized into exhibiting some of his photogenic drawings at the Royal Institution, where they were introduced by Michael Faraday. A week later he exhibited them at the Royal Society, this time himself delivering a hastily written paper entitled "Some Account of the Art of Photogenic Drawing; or the Process by Which Nature's Objects May Be Made to Delineate Themselves Without the Aid of the Artist's Pencil."[*] Apparently envious of Daguerre's popular success, he at last worked on enlarging and improving his pictures by using bigger cameras and on cutting down the lengthy exposure time. But even his friend Herschel told him that his results were inferior to daguerreotypes, writing of these from Paris:

> It is hardly too much to call them miraculous. Certainly they surpass anything I could have conceived as within the bounds of reasonable expectation. The most elaborate engraving falls far short of the richness and delicacy of execution, every gradation of light and shade is given with a softness and fidelity which sets all painting at an immeasurable distance. His *times* are also very short—In a bright day 3m. suffices . . . In short if you have a few days at your disposition I cannot commend you better than to *come and see* . . . The pictures are on very thin sheets of plated copper, neither expensive nor very cumbersome.[†]

Most people in these very early days must have seen photographs merely as a way of recording reality rather than any kind of artistic endeavour, and to them nothing could have rivalled the daguerreotype, with its accurate metallic rendering of sharp detail. Full details of how to make daguerreotypes were announced, as we have noted, in Paris in August 1839, and the process was demonstrated in London in September.

The Latent Image

Up to this point, Fox Talbot had, like Niépce, exposed sensitized material in his camera until an image appeared; this was then fixed chemically. But Daguerre had hit on the fact that something was actually recorded in the camera *before* it was observed by the human

[*] Published in *The Athenaeum*, London, February 9th, 1839, and in *London and Edinburgh Philosophical Magazine*, XIV, May 1839.
[†] Herschel to Fox Talbot, May 9th, 1839. Quoted by Dr. D. B. Thomas in his indispensable Science Museum monograph *The First Negatives* (Her Majesty's Stationery Office, London, 1964).

eye, something which could subsequently be revealed by chemical treatment (he used mercury vapour). He had discovered the so-called latent image, and this, together with better lenses and chemistry, enabled him to cut down exposure times dramatically—from his original twenty or thirty minutes to the three minutes quoted by Herschel. This not only improved the clarity of his results but also enabled him to capture the likeness of human beings, who could not be expected to keep still during the long exposures previously needed.

In England, Fox Talbot, utilizing the Reverend J. B. Reade's discovery that gallic acid speeds up the action of sensitized paper, made the same advance in 1840. Now that he needed to expose his pictures for less than three minutes, he too could include human beings in them. He patented the new kind of photograph in February 1841 and christened it the calotype (Greek *kalos*, "beautiful"). For a time, it was also occasionally known as the Talbotype, after its inventor. But whatever it was called, it was the most beautiful photographic process of the nineteenth century.

The calotype process requires a sheet of ordinary writing paper, preferably smooth-surfaced and close-grained, sensitized by being dipped first into solutions of nitrate of silver and iodide of potassium, which combine to coat the paper with silver iodide, and then into a solution of gallonitrate of silver (a mixture of Reade's gallic acid with silver nitrate and acetic acid). The sensitized paper—preferably slightly damp—is exposed in the camera for between thirty seconds and five minutes, preferably in bright sunlight, washed again in gallonitrate of silver, and fixed. The resulting negatives are often waxed to make them fully transparent (this was suggested to Fox Talbot by Herschel), and positives are then made on sensitized paper by direct contact printing in a printing frame (thus these are always the same size as the negatives from which they are made) and by sunlight. The positives are processed in exactly the same way as the negatives, and fixed.

Actually, the calotype never really became popular with photographers, despite the fact that it was now as fast as the daguerreotype and, being paper-based, had many advantages over it. Partly this was the result of the fascination exerted by the tiny details always discernible in daguerreotypes, partly it was because of the immense publicity earned by Daguerre for being first in the field. But mostly it stemmed from the restrictions placed by Fox Talbot on the professional use of his process. As an American manual of 1849 put it: "He is a man of some wealth, I believe, but he demands so high a price for a single right . . . that none can be found who have the temerity to purchase."* Perhaps Fox Talbot thought he would lose control over his invention once people realized how cheap the materials were that it required and how easy the process was to learn. Perhaps he was simply jealous of the recognition and riches heaped upon Daguerre. But whatever the reason, he certainly held back the practice of calotypy, especially by professionals, and its peak of perfection was reached in Scotland, where he did not take out a patent.

The Calotype Comes to Scotland

Fox Talbot, who had been made a Fellow of the Royal Society at the age of thirty-one, was a friend and correspondent of many distinguished scientists. The closest of these were Sir John Herschel, whose contribution we have already seen, and Sir David Brewster (1781–1868), a founder-member of the British Association for the Advancement of Science. Brewster's scientific talents had first shown themselves when, as a boy of ten, he had made a working telescope, and much of his later experimental work was connected with optical discoveries and inventions. Most well-known of these are the kaleidoscope (from which he made no money, since his 1816 patent was not registered properly) and the lenticular stereoscope. From 1838 to 1859, Brewster was Principal of the United Colleges of St. Salvator and St. Leonard, St. Andrews University, in Fifeshire, Scotland. Fox Talbot kept him informed of all the developments in his photographic experiments, sending him early in 1839 some examples of photogenic drawings, which Brewster exhibited at the Literary and Philosophical Society of St. Andrews. Brewster acquired a daguerreotype camera and, in January 1840, wrote and asked for details of exactly how to achieve results like Fox Talbot's: "I believe I possess everything you have written on the subject and yet I feel that I could not produce anything like your present specimens."†

As soon as Fox Talbot had discovered the latent image in September 1840, he informed Brewster in a letter, but he did not send the requested details of how to make the calotypes until May 1841,

*Henry H. Snelling, *The History and Practice of the Art of Photography; or the Production of Pictures Through the Agency of Light* (G. P. Putnam, New York, 1849, republished in facsimile, Morgan & Morgan, New York, 1970).

†Unless otherwise specified, all correspondence with Fox Talbot quoted in this section is in the Fox Talbot archives, presented to the Science Museum, London, by his granddaughter Matilda Talbot in 1937.

after he had safely taken out his English patent (No. 8842, Photographic Pictures, February 8th, 1841). He then also sent some of the essential gallic acid, which could not be bought in Scotland. Though Brewster himself did not manage to produce any calotypes, one of the two colleagues to whom he passed on the information and chemicals was Dr. John Adamson (1810–70), who was at various times Curator of the College Museum in St. Andrews and Professor of Chemistry there. He produced the first calotypes in Scotland in 1841, and Brewster sent some samples to Fox Talbot in November. By March 1842 Fox Talbot was able to tell him that he thought Adamson's results excellent, though Brewster's other colleague, Major Hugh Playfair, did not have any success at this time.

An album of John Adamson's calotypes, which he left to his son when he died, was given to the Royal Scottish Museum, Edinburgh, in 1942 by his grandson W. P. H. Tulloch, along with one of his photographic scrapbooks. On page 42 of this album are the negative and positive of a portrait of Miss Melville Adamson, one of John and Robert's sisters, who appears in Hill and Adamson's calotype of the Adamson family (figure 3). The negative is captioned, in John Adamson's own writing:

3. The Adamson family—page 229.

> This negative calotype was taken in the spring of 1841 by Mr. Fox Talbot's process, and before he had made it public—he explained the process in a letter to Sir D. Brewster, and this picture was obtained by following his directions and using a temporary camera obscura made with a common small lens or burning glass an inch and a half in diameter—it is no doubt the first calotype portrait taken in Scotland. The sitting lasted nearly two minutes in bright sunshine.

The picture is dated "May 1840," and the "1841" in the long caption has been altered to "1840." It is probable, however, from the sequence of events described, that "1840" is a mistake of later years, for Brewster had written to Fox Talbot in July 1841: "Dr. Adamson, who is a good Chemist and successful with the Daguerreotype, has also failed, and says that the paper when ready for the camera becomes black in the dark.

Brewster had advised Fox Talbot that it would not be financially worthwhile to go to the trouble of patenting his process in Scotland and, early in 1842, Fox Talbot wrote to ask if anyone in that country might be persuaded to take calotypes professionally, to compete with the all-conquering daguerreotypes. At that time there were less than a dozen licensed users of Fox Talbot's process in England. John Adamson's younger brother, Robert, a delicate twenty-one-year-old with weak lungs, was extremely interested in mechanics and spent most of his spare time making models of steam engines, wheel-barrows, and boats, which he sailed on the stream alongside the Adamson family home at Burnside, St. Andrews. He had been apprenticed for a year or two to a millwright in nearby Cupar, but his constitution was found not to be strong enough for such hard work; it seems likely that he suffered from tuberculosis, but there is no evidence for this even in the Register entry of his early death—information about Robert Adamson's life is not easy to come by. To his family, photography must have seemed a heaven-sent answer to the very difficult problem of finding him a career. In August 1842 Brewster was able to tell Fox Talbot that "A brother of Dr. Adamson . . . is willing to practise the calotype in Edinburgh as a profession. Mr. Adamson . . . has been well drilled in the new art by his brother."

In that month of August, Robert had taken his first pictures (some, initialled "R. A." and dated "1842," are in the Gernsheim Collection), and on November 9th, 1842, John Adamson sent an album to Fox Talbot, with a covering letter:

4. Robert Adamson's first calotype (Royal Scottish Museum, Edinburgh).

> I take the liberty of sending you a few Calotypes executed by myself and brother in testimony of the great pleasure we have derived from your discovery—I hope they will not be devoid of interest from the objects which they picture, whatever may be their rank as specimens of the art.*

By January 1843 the *Edinburgh Review* was reporting:

> We have now before us a collection of admirable photographs executed by *Dr. and Mr. Robert Adamson, Major Playfair* and *Captain Brewster.* Several of these have all the force and beauty of the Sketches of Rembrandt, and some of them have been pronounced by Mr. Talbot himself to be among the best he has seen . . . All these calotypes were taken by means of the excellent camera obscuras constructed by Mr. Thomas Davidson, optician in Edinburgh . . . Mr. Robert Adamson, whose skill and experience in photography is very great, is about to practise the art professionally in our northern metropolis.

*Letter now in the possession of the Fox Talbot Museum, Lacock.

On May 9th, Brewster wrote to Fox Talbot to tell him that "Mr. Adamson, of whom I have previously written to you, goes tomorrow to Edinburgh to prosecute, as a Profession, the Calotype."* In Edinburgh, Robert Adamson installed himself in the small eighteenth-century Rock House, Calton Stairs, Calton Hill, and, on July 3rd, Brewster wrote again to Fox Talbot: "Mr. Adamson, who is now established in Edin[burgh] with crowds every day at his Studio, will be very grateful for your kindness. He will send you specimens of his progress which I think will delight and surprise you."† In the same month Hugh Miller, editor of *The Witness* and later a much-photographed friend of Hill and Adamson, published an article on the calotype in that magazine in which he "recommends a visit to the Studio of Mr. Adamson and urges the encouragement of his art."

Paper photography had arrived in Scotland, and it had already become professional. But Brewster and his friends kept up their amateur interest through the newly founded Calotype Club (there was later a quite unconnected one in London), which met regularly in Edinburgh, mainly to take pictures of the city architecture and landscapes. As well as Brewster himself, the members were Sheriff Cosmo Innes, Professor Moir, Sheriff Tennant, Sheriff Mark Napier, Dean Montgomery, John Stewart, and Sheriff Cary. On July 3rd, Brewster asked Fox Talbot for "specimens of your Calotype [because] I have the largest collection in Scotland, and whenever I go to Edin[burgh], I carry a series along with which to delight the dilettants there."

D.O. HILL AND

THE DISRUPTION OF

THE CHURCH OF SCOTLAND

David Octavius Hill (1802–70) was born into a large family ("Octavius" signifying the eighth child) in Perth, a pleasant little town sometimes known as the "Fair City," at the head of the Firth of Tay, some forty miles north of Edinburgh. In its fifteenth-century chapel

* Also in the possession of the Fox Talbot Museum.
†Letter from Brewster to Fox Talbot, July 3rd, 1843, now in the Science Museum, London, and first exhibited publicly in the National Portrait Gallery's exhibition "The Hill / Adamson Albums," March / April, 1973.

John Knox preached his famous sermon against idolatry. Hill's parents were Emilia (née Murray) and Thomas, who ran a stationer's business at 6 George Street. Thomas also dealt in books and prints, as later did David's brother Alexander. The boys were educated at Perth Academy, with which their father had for some time been connected and which was said to have, under its headmaster Adam Anderson, as high an academic standard at that period, especially in mathematics, chemistry, and physics, as any university in Scotland. Alexander, the elder of the two, achieved some distinction there and went on to a career in publishing, becoming head clerk of the famous Edinburgh firm of Blackwood's in 1821, before starting his own business. At about the same time, David went to Edinburgh to study at the Trustees' Academy School of Design in Picardy Place under Andrew Wilson, the influential painter, teacher, and connoisseur, who was a considerable power in Scottish art galleries and institutions until he went to live in Italy in 1826.

Hill learnt the comparatively new art of lithography and, from 1821 to 1823, his *Sketches of Scenery in Perthshire drawn from Nature and on Stone by D. O. Hill* was published in six parts by his father and distributed by Blackwood's. Not only was this work a very early example of lithography in Britain, but it was an extremely ambitious undertaking for so young a man, only nineteen when the first issue appeared. Hill, as much of what he did in later life was to show, was nothing if not energetic and ambitious. In 1823, as the last part came out, three of his paintings on which he had based lithographs were exhibited at the Royal Institution for the Promotion of the Fine Arts in Scotland, Edinburgh's chief centre for exhibitions, founded three years earlier. These, his earliest known oils, were *Dunkeld, near Perth, at Sunset* and two views of the Tay at Perth. For the next twenty years, the main inspiration for his painting was the scenery of his native land. It was a romantic age, and a love of wild and majestic mountain landscapes, with mysterious glens, lofty trees, and glowing sunsets, was shared by most of Hill's contemporaries.

Hill was to become important to Scotland's artistic life not only as a practitioner but as an organizer. When a number of Scottish painters became disillusioned with the aims of the Royal Institution for the Promotion of the Fine Arts (which Hill had joined in 1826), they established an independent Society of Artists in 1829. Hill was a founder-member, and in 1830 became its second secretary, serving for several years without salary. He began to receive payment for his work in 1836 and remained secretary for almost forty years. When ill health forced Hill to resign in 1869, the grateful members voted to continue his salary for the rest of his life. The Society of Artists became the Royal Scottish Academy of Fine Arts by royal charter granted in 1839 and in due course took over the functions—and even the premises—of the Royal Institution itself.

Hill's own work concentrated more and more on book illustration. In 1831 and 1832, for instance, he prepared illustrations for *The Abbot*, *Redgauntlet*, and *The Fair Maid of Perth* for the first collected edition of Sir Walter Scott's Waverley Novels, published by Robert Cadell (page 362). Soon after this, he was commissioned to paint fourteen landscapes as illustrations for an eight-volume edition of *The Works of Robert Burns*. This led to the most famous book illustrated by Hill, *The Land of Burns*, published in two volumes at Hill's instigation by John Blackie in 1840, with a commentary by "Christopher North," *nom de plume* of the man who appears in the National Portrait Gallery albums as Professor John Wilson of Edinburgh University (figure 5). Hill painted for the book sixty-one Scottish scenes connected with the life and poetry of Burns, and many of these were exhibited at the Royal Scottish Academy. The whole enterprise was such an enormous critical and popular success that Hill and Blackie decided to set up a permanent Burns museum near the poet's birthplace in Ayrshire, with Hill's paintings as the main attraction. But they failed to raise sufficient funds and, though the scheme remained in their minds for many years, it finally died when a fire destroyed most of the paintings in the 1860's.

On August 9th, 1837, after a long engagement, Hill married his first wife, Ann Macdonald, the musically inclined daughter of a Perth wine merchant. The fact that the Society of Artists finally had been able to give him a salary in 1836 decided Hill that he could at last afford to marry, and for a few years he and his wife kept house on Moray Place, in the New Town, then and now the most fashionable quarter of Edinburgh. Here they entertained the art world of Scotland and led a happy and sociable life. In January 1839 they had a daughter, Charlotte, but a second girl, born in 1840, lived only two hours. Mrs. Hill became more and more an invalid, and while Hill kept up his full life of painting and administration at the Royal Scottish Academy, she played an ever-decreasing role, until she died some short time thereafter. The family home, now moved to 28 Inverleith

5. *Professor John Wilson—page 196.*

Row, was no longer a centre of modish dinners and soirées for the fashionable elite of Edinburgh, and soon Hill went to live with his widowed sister Mary Watson (figure 6) at 6 Pitt Street.

6. Mrs. Mary Watson—page 225.

The Disruption

On May 18th, 1843, Hill was present at a dramatic event in the history of the Scottish Church. It is not clear whether he was there because he was interested in Church affairs, or because his brother-in-law, Dr. Macdonald, was minister of North Leith, or merely because the event seems to have been a great spectacle, watched by eager crowds. What *is* clear is that he was deeply moved by the resignation of one hundred fifty-five ministers from the Church of Scotland, who walked out of the General Assembly to march downhill through the steep streets of Edinburgh's New Town to a specially improvised assembly room at Tanfield Hall, Canonmills, not far from Hill's Inverleith Row studio.

When the Church of Scotland was founded in the sixteenth century, John Knox, its first leader, had established the right of each congregation to accept or reject its own ministers. This right had been repealed early in the eighteenth century, in the reign of Queen Anne, then successively granted and withdrawn again. In 1834 the Veto Act had finally removed the congregations' right of choice, and the so-called Disruption of 1843 was the culmination of a ten-year crescendo of revolt against the interference of the Crown and the landowners in the patronage and livings of the Scottish Church. After listening to the Act of Protest read out by the Moderator, Dr. David Welsh (figure 7), and walking out of the General Assembly, the dissident ministers established at Tanfield Hall the Free Church of Scotland. Five days later they returned to Tanfield to sign the Deed of Demission marking their break from the old Church (to which, to keep things in proportion, it should be noted that seven hundred fifty-two ministers remained loyal). The dissidents grew daily in numbers, encouraged by the extraordinary achievements of the new Church. Twenty-five years later, these were listed as follows:

7. The Reverend Dr. David Welsh—page 77.

The Free Church of Scotland, since her separation from the Establishment in 1843 when nearly 500 clergymen voluntarily resigned their homes and livings, has built 900 Churches, 650 Manses, 3 Theological Colleges, 2 Normal or Training Institutions, 500 Schools. Her average income for the three years previous to 1868 has been £370,000 and during the 25 years of existence without State support, the sum raised by her amounts to over EIGHT MILLIONS STERLING.*

The events at Tanfield Hall were, as a Scottish ecclesiastical historian has pointed out,† carefully calculated to impress spectators: "This first Free Assembly met to demonstrate rather than to deliberate. It was characterised by a spectacular element which, like the inaugural procession, made a very vivid appeal to the people at large." Among those most impressed was Hill, who determined to paint a monumental commemorative picture of the type made popular by his English contemporaries Benjamin Robert Haydon and Sir George Hayter. The latter's most famous work in the genre, *The Great Reform Bill, 1832*, may even have been seen by Hill only days before, since it was only completed and put on display at the Egyptian Hall, Piccadilly, London, in April 1843, though it had been begun ten years earlier. It was on show in Edinburgh in November, where one of those who saw it was John Harden (figure 8): " . . . take a walk to see Hayter's splendidly painted picture of the Interior of the House of Commons, with 400 portraits (from life) & his studies of portraits from life to make his reduced picture groups—a wonderful production 10 years labour. Extremely cleverly done, but a formal, insipid subject marvellously treated—" (letter to his daughter Jessie, November 14th, 1843).

8. *John Harden—page 138.*

Though Hill started to make composition sketches for his painting immediately, it soon became clear to him that the major problem was how to record the faces of the nearly five hundred ministers involved. Hayter had had the same trouble with *The Great Reform Bill*, and four years after he had started work *The Times* of June 29th, 1837, admonished some of the parliamentarians involved thus: "It is desirable that those gentlemen who have promised the artist to sit, in order that he may lose no time in finishing his arduous task, will not delay to redeem their promises." For Hill, the situation was made worse by the fact that he was by training and experience a landscape painter; only one portrait by him dating from before the

* From the caption to carbon reproductions of Hill's Disruption Painting; see page 46.
† J.R. Fleming, D.D., *A History of the Church in Scotland, 1843–1874* (T. & T. Clark, Edinburgh, 1927).

Disruption is known, an oil (figure 9), now in the Perth Art Gallery, of his father, who died in 1826.

Once again, Sir David Brewster plays a decisive part in the story. He had originally intended to make his career in the Church and had been an ordained minister for nearly forty years, preaching regularly in Edinburgh, Leith, and elsewhere from 1804 onwards. He had taken part in every stage of the "long conflict," as the revolt against patronage in the Scottish Church was called, had signed the Act of Protest, and "come out" of the General Assembly on May 18th with his elder brother, the Reverend James Brewster of Craig (figure 10). He attended every session of the first Free Church Assembly * and, when he heard of Hill's intentions, suggested to him that the new art of photography was the ideal way of obtaining the huge number of portraits involved. In the letter of July 3rd, 1843, quoted above, he wrote to Fox Talbot:

> You may probably have heard . . . of the great event in Scotland, of 500 Ministers quitting their *Manses* & *Glebes* & *Stipends* for Conscience sake, and forming a Free Church, unshackled by secular interferences. A grand historical picture is undertaken by a first rate Artist, to represent the *first General Assembly of the Free Church.* I got hold of the artist—showed him the Calotype, & the eminent advantage he might derive from it in getting likenesses of all the principal characters before they dispersed to their respective homes. He was at first incredulous, but went to Mr. Adamson, and arranged with him preliminaries for getting all the necessary portraits.

9. Thomas Hill (Perth Art Gallery, Scotland).

10. The Reverend Dr. James Brewster—page 84.

HILL AND ADAMSON:

A WORKING PARTNERSHIP

So began the great collaboration between David Octavius Hill and Robert Adamson, and it did so with the fairly humble aim of using photographs as reference material for a painter to work from. This has always been an important stimulus to the use of photography; famous nineteenth-century examples are the 1884 photograph of W. E. Gladstone by Rupert Potter, father of Beatrix, in the pose used by John Millais in his portrait in oils now at Christ Church, Oxford,

*This led, within a fortnight, to an unsuccessful attempt by the Established Presbyterian Church to expel him from his post of principal at St. Andrews University.

and Étienne Carjat's 1863 photograph of Charles Baudelaire that many years later became the basis of Georges Rouault's oil painting.

The most striking example in the National Portrait Gallery albums is the calotype of the English painter William Etty (figure 11), taken while the painter and his family were visiting Edinburgh from October 16th to 18th, 1844, for a Royal Scottish Academy dinner in Etty's honour (Etty may also have met Hill a few days earlier, when the latter was in York for the meeting of the British Association for the Advancement of Science). The Etty calotype was used as a basis for two almost identical paintings, one in the National Portrait Gallery and the other in the Art Gallery of the City of York (where Etty was born). These were for a long time thought to be self-portraits, but, as Richard Ormond writes in his *Catalogue of Early Victorian Portraits in the National Portrait Gallery* (Her Majesty's Stationery Office, London, 1973), "They are . . . of poor quality, and their entire dependence on the Hill and Adamson calotype photograph . . . suggests the work of a copyist." Both are careful and unimaginative copies of the photograph reproduced in this book, one of two in existence that were obviously taken at the same sitting. Like many of the later examples of photography used for artists' reference, the photographs are here clearly much more effective and forcefully true to life than the paintings based on them.

11. William Etty—page 122.

Hill and Adamson must have taken to each other almost at once. Even while giving Fox Talbot his July news of the collaboration, Brewster could report: "They have succeeded beyond their most sanguine expectations—Groups of 25 persons in the same picture all placed in attitudes which the Painter desired, and very large pictures beside have been taken of each individual to assist the Painter in the completion of his Picture." Brewster had "seen one of the groups of 25 persons with our distinguished Moderator Dr. Chalmers sitting in the heart of them, and I have never seen anything finer." This is presumably the calotype described by Hugh Miller, in the article from *The Witness* quoted from above, as being on display at Alexander Hill's print shop in July 1843.

So successfully did the forty-one-year-old painter and his young colleague get on that they soon decided not to restrict themselves to the purposes of the Disruption painting. Brewster again (July 3rd):

> Mr. D. O. Hill the Painter is in the act of entering into partnership with Mr. Adamson, and proposes to apply the Calotype to many other general purposes of a very popular kind, and es-

pecially to the execution of large pictures representing diff. bodies & classes of individuals. I think you will find that we have, in Scotland, found out the value of your invention not before yourself, but before those to whom you have given the privilege of using it.

This very quick decision on a partnership reinforces the impression that Hill and Adamson found a way of working together immediately. It appears that, as would be appropriate to their respective qualifications, Hill arranged the sitters, the costumes, and the backgrounds, while Adamson looked after the cameras and the chemical processes. This is reflected in the description of the first calotypes they showed at the Royal Scottish Academy of Arts in 1844 as "Executed by R. Adamson under the artistic direction of D. O. Hill." Eight portraits were exhibited: Sir William Allan, President of the Royal Scottish Academy from 1837 to 1850; the Reverend J. Julius Wood; Sir David Brewster; Thomas Duncan; C. E. Stewart; Mr. Williamson; George Meikle Kemp; and "A Lady." Pictures of the first four are in Volume I of the National Portrait Gallery albums and are included in this volume.

By the following year, 1845, Hill and Adamson's description of the works exhibited at the Royal Scottish Academy had changed to "Calotype Portrait Sketches, designed and arranged by D. O. Hill and executed by R. Adamson" and the number had jumped to fifty-two. These included many in Volume I of the National Portrait Gallery albums (Lord Robertson, Dr. George Cook, the Reverend Andrew Gray, William Etty, John Stevens, et al.), as well as "A New-haven Fisher-woman" and "A Newhaven Pilot." In 1846 they showed "A frame of Calotype Studies." There is some reason to suppose that some of Hill's painter friends took a hand in the "artistic direction" of the calotypes. John Harden (figure 8), the amateur Lakeland painter who was photographed while visiting his son Robert in Edinburgh, wrote to his daughter Jessie: "Sir Wm [William] Allan arranged my standing attitude." It is difficult to believe that the other artists who visited Rock House did not sometimes also pose the sitters they found there.

Of course, during these years Hill was still secretary of the Royal Scottish Academy and was showing paintings at its exhibitions (as he did every year until 1860, for a grand total of nearly three hundred paintings and drawings, a handful of which were also shown at the Royal Academy in London). Amongst those listed in 1846, for in-

*12. Durham Cathedral—pages 330–1;
see also pages 334–5.*

stance, is one of Durham Cathedral, perhaps based on the photographs. It is surprising that such a link between the calotypes and Hill's paintings does not occur more often. He was, after all, primarily a painter of landscapes and might have been expected to use his new-found source of reference material more frequently to help him with these. But apart from this possible connection of the Durham calotypes with a painting (Hill also exhibited a view of Durham Cathedral at the Royal Scottish Academy in 1853), the only other examples in the National Portrait Gallery albums are the two pictures of Linlithgow (figure 13 and pages 332–3), which were probably taken for a painting of that town commissioned from Hill by John Miller, the engineer of the Glasgow and Garnkirk Railway and close friend of the artist. There also exists—though not in the National Portrait Gallery albums—a series of photographs of Ballochmyle railway viaduct, which led to the painting of it now in the Museum of Transport, Glasgow, one of a series of West Lothian scenes commissioned by Miller, who designed that viaduct and several others.

13. Linlithgow Palace—page 329.

Finally, Miller, who on his death owned eight Hill paintings, commissioned a view of Edinburgh from the Castle, for which Hill and Adamson made reference calotypes in August 1846. When the resulting oil was first exhibited, it was much praised for its accuracy, which obviously owed a good deal to the photographs, but in general it seems that for landscapes Hill was sufficiently confident of his skill in capturing topographical details not to feel the need of calotype images to work from, whereas he was clearly less certain about his ability to capture the contours of the human face. Adamson, too, had a problem: the best calotypes were made with the sensitized paper being still wet when placed in the camera. Photographs taken at or near his Edinburgh residence, Rock House, would always be most likely to meet his technical demands.

Nevertheless, photography soon became Hill's major preoccupation, and within a few months of going into partnership with Adamson he, too, moved into Rock House—which had two floors and several attics for living and working—in order to devote more time to it. From there the partners produced, in only four and a half years of concentrated effort, at least fifteen hundred photographs. This is the figure usually quoted, because about fourteen hundred paper negatives are known to have survived, but the total number was probably at least twice as many. They clearly made many different exposures at each portrait sitting, for instance, not only to have alternative poses available, but to ensure that there was always a

14. James Spence (Private Collection).

satisfactory negative to print from. Probably what they most feared was the possibility of a shot being ruined through the sitter having moved during the long minute or so he or she was required to keep quite still, and many of the pictures which survive as negatives but not as prints show precisely this failing. It is, naturally enough, usually the face which is blurred.

Many of their calotypes in different collections hitherto thought of as duplicates can, when placed side by side, be recognized as slightly different versions of the same subject. The Scottish National Portrait Gallery, for instance, which has the largest collection of Hill and Adamson negatives (about nine hundred), has a set of no less than nine differently posed pictures, sitting and standing, of James Spence (figure 14), the surgeon who in 1864 succeeded James Miller (pages 101, 214) as Professor of Surgery at Edinburgh University. No two are quite the same, yet all could quite easily have been taken at the same session.

Many of the portraits taken by Hill and Adamson are included in the National Portrait Gallery albums and reproduced in this book. Indeed, Volume I of the albums is entirely made up of photographs of individuals (except for the usual decorative frontispiece showing a tomb in Greyfriars Churchyard, four pictures with two people in each, and one with three), and it is because this volume appeared to be in better condition than any other presentation album of Hill and Adamson calotypes that it seemed so important for it to be in the National Portrait Gallery.

At first sight, all the portraits look as if they were taken in a studio, or at least indoors, but in this respect it is a misnomer to talk of Rock House as a "studio," although that is exactly what Hill and Adamson did call it: their later prints were mounted on cards which bore the printed line "Published by D. O. Hill and Robert Adamson at their Calotype Studio, Calton Stairs, Edinburgh." However, despite the improvements made by Fox Talbot in his process, the materials used were still rather insensitive, and to keep exposures down to a minute or so, strong sunlight was required. So the furniture and properties needed for the picture were arranged in the open air outside the southwest front of Rock House to obtain a convincing illusion of an interior. A close look at many of the portraits will reveal clues to this; for instance, in the pictures of Mrs. Rigby (see figure 15) one can see the stone outer wall of the house with ivy growing up it on the left-hand side of the picture, and a curtain from inside the house draped on the right. Or again, Miss

15. Mrs. Anne Rigby—page 115;
see also pages 108, 109, 110, 114, 116.

16. Elizabeth Logan—page 281;
see also pages 280, 282.

Elizabeth Logan (figure 16) apparently sleeps on a cushion indoors in a carefully composed setting of furniture, a curtain, a fallen fruit basket, and a ball. But into the top and left of the picture intrudes— again—that ivy.

This dependence on sunlight makes the total number of pictures Hill and Adamson took in four and a half years remarkable, though it is clear from the dating of some of the negatives that they must have made use of every available day of winter sunshine that occurred. One way in which they intensified the available light was by using a mirror to reflect light on to the sitter, especially on to his face. This technique is today frequently used on film sets but much more rarely by still photographers. One of the mirrors apparently used in this way by Hill and Adamson is now in the museum of the Royal Photographic Society in London, to which it was given by the famous Impressionist photographer Alvin Langdon Coburn, who got it from his friend J. Craig Annan, photographer son of Thomas Annan. This was, like the cameras and lenses they used, made by Thomas Davidson, who was himself something of a daguerreotypist and manufactured the first symmetrical doublet lens. In a letter to the *Liverpool and Manchester Photographic Journal* in October 1859, when he lived in Newcastle upon Tyne, Davidson wrote: "I also made a speculum of 24-inch diameter and 30-inch focus . . . for taking smaller portraits or to reflect light on the object, but that was never much used." This would seem to be the object which came into Coburn's hands.

Despite this ingenuity, Hill and Adamson often had to give the negatives far too long an exposure time to reasonably expect their sitters to sit still. It was fortunate that the kind of pose suggested to Hill by his artistic training and academic knowledge as being tasteful and appropriate for a portrait should involve placing the sitter so that he was able to lean on his hands, the arm of a chair, a heavy book, or a stick (or, as seems to have been more fashionable, an umbrella), for all these made excellent supports for helping the sitters to hold their breath and keep absolutely still.

Hill and Adamson also sometimes used a tripod or headrest similar to those which later became standard equipment in portrait studios and were widely advertised in catalogues of equipment available to the profession. Usually, of course, the sitter would be posed so that the tripod was not visible on the final picture but sometimes, as can be seen on the original retouched negative, this was miscalculated. A very clear example is the portrait of the Reverend J. Julius

17. Fisher Laddies—page 191.

Wood (page 81), where even in the print one can just see that a tripod has been painted over in the top left-hand corner; in the negative, the retouching can be seen much more clearly. In a more striking case, "Fisher Laddies" (figure 17), not only can the shape of the tripod easily be discerned in the top and bottom right-hand corners of the print, but one leg of it has been overlooked altogether and is clearly seen sticking out from the right knee of the boy on the right. This retouching should, of course, have been done on the negative. Because it was not, the protruding leg is visible on all the prints of this picture that I have seen.

Hill's expertise in painting was of great assistance in this retouching process. Nearly a third of the original negatives in the Scottish National Portrait Gallery's collection show some evidence of retouching, usually far more skilful and unobtrusive than in the two examples I have cited. Sometimes only the watermark on the paper they most commonly used—Whatman's Turkey Mill—has been made less obvious (it can still often be discerned on the original prints). Detail in clothing or background that has not come out clearly is sketched in, skies are lightened, flowers are revived, patterns are strengthened. In some portraits of ministers, lettering is filled in on the books they are carrying to identify their churches; in the picture of the Reverend J. Julius Wood (page 81) the cover of the book in the original negative is blank.

But it is important to point out that, as far as one can see, Hill never altered the face or features of the sitter, which was always the most forceful and telling part of each picture. The face was obviously sacred to him, and his retouching is therefore quite honest, a very different business from the wholesale prettifying of sitters that started with the upsurge of studio photography in the 1850's and has only fairly recently become the exception rather than the rule.

The partners did not confine their activities to Rock House. Their first excursion was probably to Glasgow in October 1843, where, at the first Assembly of the Free Church of Scotland, they took advantage of the breaks in the sessions to photograph groups of ministers. By the end of December they had otained in this manner, or in single portraits, about one third of the necessary photographs. Almost a year later they were at York Museum to record the scientists attending a meeting of the British Association for the Advancement of Science (Dr. James Inglis, specialist in the treatment of goitre, and the Marquis of Northampton, President of the Royal Society, were photographed there). It was possibly on the same trip that they

18. Dr. James Inglis—page 210.

19. The Marquis of Northampton—page 195.

photographed Durham Cathedral, as Lady Eastlake's journal for December 19th, 1844, reads: "To Mr. Hill's to see his wonderful calotypes—one of Durham most exquisite."[*]

They frequently went to Bonaly Tower, Colinton, about twenty miles southeast of Rock House, whose owner, Lord Cockburn, a judge, had been a friend of Hill's ever since they were both involved in the formation of the Royal Scottish Academy. He had been a patron and supporter, too, since the first scheme to paint the Disruption, of which he said, "There has not been such a subject since the days of Knox and not then."[†]

20. John Knox's House—page 245.

Hill and Adamson took many pictures of the splendid picnics at Bonaly, especially in the unusually hot summers of 1846 and 1847, and Lord Cockburn's interest in such activities and in photography continued after they had stopped work. In his *Circuit Journeys* he wrote, "Knockomie, Saturday night, 15th September, 1849. This day . . . was driven to Pluscarden, nine miles off . . . we loitered about the ruin for some hours, and had a turf refection, and a good deal of calotyping, conducted by my good friend, Cosmo Innes, the Sheriff of the county."[‡] Cosmo Innes, it will be remembered, was one of the members of the Calotype Club at the beginning of the 1840's.

Lord Cockburn was also something of a conservationist (the Cockburn Association existed to promote the architectural beauties and amenities of Edinburgh) and later in his life was much involved in the losing battle to prevent Waverley Station and its associated railway lines from taking up some thirteen acres of the land between Princes Street and the Castle. A more successful campaign prevented the demolition of John Knox's house at 45 High Street, on the Royal Mile, threatened in 1844. Hill and Adamson's calotype of the sixteenth-century house, taken at about that time (figure 20), may well have been made at Cockburn's instigation.

21. Greyfriars Churchyard—page 236; see also pages 234–44.

A quarter of a mile from John Knox's house is Greyfriars Churchyard (figure 21), which appealed to Hill and Adamson as much as it had earlier to the members of the Calotype Club and as it was to do later to Thomas Keith, a friend of Hill's who made excellent calotypes of Edinburgh architecture and the surrounding country-

[*]*Journal and Correspondence of Lady Eastlake*, edited by her nephew Charles Eastlake Smith (John Murray, London, 1895).

[†]Quoted in the offer for sale of the photographs of *The Disruption of the Church of Scotland: An Historical Picture (Containing Four Hundred and Fifty Portraits) Representing the Signing of the Deed of Demission by the Ministers of the First General Assembly of the Free Church* (Schenk & McFarlane, Edinburgh, 1866).

[‡]Lord Cockburn, *Circuit Journeys* (David Douglas, Edinburgh, 1888, 2nd edition 1889).

side in the early 1850's. Though a dozen of Hill and Adamson's pictures of tombs in the churchyard appear in the National Portrait Gallery albums, there are curiously none of their other favourite Edinburgh subject, the Castle and its garrison of the 92nd Highlanders (the Gordons), a large number of which were taken in August 1845.

The Portraits

The calotype was the ideal medium for portraiture, since its results could not be achieved with the daguerreotype, which, although superb at recording minutiae, had metallic qualities which made subtle effects difficult; it could not even be looked at properly except in the right light. As Brewster wrote to Fox Talbot (July 3rd, 1843): "The Daguerreotype is considered infinitely inferior for all practical purposes, notwithstanding its beauty and sharpness," and Hill himself wrote: "The rough and unequal texture throughout the paper is the main cause of the calotype failing in details before the Daguerreotype . . . and this is the very life of it. They look like the imperfect work of man . . . and not the much diminished perfect work of God."* John Harden (figure 8) wrote, "I am much interested in that splendid discovery in the Arts & Ex. *great* improvement on Daguerreotype called Calotype . . . it is indeed a marvellously great advance in Art & Scientific discovery (A Mr Talbotts [sic]) see the Edinbro' Review for January last for a descriptive account—the pictures produced are as Rembrandt's but improved so like his style & the oldest & finest masters that doubtless a great progress in Portrait painting & effect must be the consequence." †

As one might guess, many of the portraits taken by Hill and Adamson, especially in the first years of their partnership, were of the ministers who were present at the Disruption of the Church of Scotland, for one must not forget—though Hill must occasionally have done so—that this was his original reason for turning to photography. Actually, the scene which he had decided to portray had changed slightly and, at the suggestion of Dr. Robert Gordon of Edinburgh High Church, he had resolved not to show the ministers listening to either Dr. Welsh, the outgoing Moderator (page 77), or

---

*Hill to Mr. Bicknell, January 17th, 1848, now in George Eastman House, Rochester, New York.
†Letter to his married daughter, Mrs. Jane Barker (perhaps the lady on page 267), November 23rd, 1843.

Dr. Thomas Chalmers (figure 22), the first Free Church Moderator, at the first Disruption Assembly in Tanfield Hall, but, more dramatically, as they signed the Deed of Demission a few days later to symbolize their renunciation of livings and homes ("In the very act of their heroic sacrifice," said Dr. Gordon). To underline this theme, the actual moment chosen was the signing of the Deed by the Reverend Patrick Macfarlan, minister of Greenock, the richest living in the Church of Scotland. Not only was he giving up more, in a material sense, than any other signatory, but "what was to his Conservative feelings much dearer and harder to part with, his position as an honoured member of his beloved Establishment." * It was, of course, a great sacrifice for everyone who took part. The Reverend Hugh McKay Mackenzie of Tongue (photographed by Hill and Adamson, although not included in these albums) "with his son the Rev. William Mackenzie, so suffered in health from the hardships of the Disruption, that they died within a month of each other in the summer of 1845."†

22. The Reverend Thomas Chalmers— page 74.

Hill's change of plan may perhaps explain why a large number of the ministers who, according to H. Scott,‡ "came out" in 1843 are not included in the final Disruption painting. Some of them were certainly photographed by Hill and Adamson, since many ministers who do not appear in the painting are represented in the National Portrait Gallery albums and elsewhere. But of those who do figure in the painting some two hundred calotypes have been identified; thirty are in the albums and are reproduced in "The Disruption Painting" section of this book.

Hill himself drew a key to his Disruption painting, and this has served as a vital guide to matching the painted faces with their photographs. When they are matched, most are seen to be in precisely the same poses, and there is even a tendency to place those faces which appear larger in the original calotypes in the foreground of the painting, and the smaller ones in the background, showing that Hill copied them almost directly on to the canvas. Since the calotype negatives, when waxed, could be printed from either side, Hill could even reverse a face when it suited his composition (for example, Master James Miller, figure 23, whose father, uncle, and grand-

23. Master James Miller—page 100; see also pages 275, 276

* The Disruption of the Church of Scotland: An Historical Picture . . .
† Rev. Thomas Brown, Annals of the Disruption (Macniven & Wallace, Edinburgh, 1884). The frontispiece is J. M. Corner's engraving of Hill's Disruption painting.
‡ Fasti Ecclesiae Scoticanae (The Succession of Ministers in the Parish Churches of Scotland from the Reformation in A.D. 1560 to the Present Time) (Oliver & Boyd, Edinburgh, 1866–71, revised edition 1915–28).

father all appear in the National Portrait Gallery albums). There is some evidence that on one or two occasions Adamson actually printed from both sides of a negative merely to illustrate its transparency—to show off his technical skill, as it were.

Even with the key and its long list of four hundred and fifty names printed underneath there are problems of identification. There are twenty-five numbered but unnamed faces in the key (often half-hidden ones) and even more that are not numbered (a simplified key to those included in this book is on pages 66–67). When writing the captions Hill sometimes could not remember who the sitters were (four portraits in Volume I of the National Portrait Gallery albums are untitled) and, even when he could, his information is not always very helpful. He describes the man on John Gibson's right in figure 24 as "Revd Mr Moir," but is this George Moir (1800–70), as is usually stated, or David Macbeth Moir (1798–1851)? Neither of them were "Reverends," but both moved in the same sort of Edinburgh society as Hill, and both wrote for *Blackwood's Magazine*. Since neither face matches the "Dr. Moir" shown in the Disruption painting, perhaps it is neither; though David Macbeth Moir *was* a doctor! Sometimes, Hill's memory is clearly just plain faulty; his caption to the photograph on page 342, for instance, reads "Mr Welsh," presumably the Reverend William Welsh, minister of Mossfennan, in the Disruption painting. But, although he does look a little like Welsh (as we know from another calotype), he looks a lot more like the Reverend Thomas Scott, a Hill and Adamson calotype of whom was shown at the Great Exhibition.

•

Hill's position in Edinburgh society brought him into contact with all the most important people, especially in the arts and academic life, who lived in the city or visited it. Many were persuaded to visit Rock House. Not only William Etty (figure 11), but Sir Francis Grant (figure 25) and David Roberts (page 141), who had gone on to earn bigger rewards and fame as painters in London were photographed in visits to Edinburgh, as was Robert Liston (figure 26), who had gone to work at the hospital attached to the University of London (University College Hospital) in 1834 and became University Professor of Clinical Surgery in 1835. Nearly all the painters and sculptors working in Scotland at the time were photographed, for Hill counted most of them as friends; some he had known since he had been at the Trustees' Academy School of Design with them, and

24. The Reverend Mr. Moir and John Gibson—page 102.

25. Sir Francis Grant—page 125.

26. Robert Liston—page 202; see also pages 203, 218.

James Ballantine (figure 27), Thomas Duncan (pages 94, 124, 139, 150, 241), John Henning (pages 78, 129, 130, 142, 146), Kenneth Macleay (page 148), Handyside Ritchie (pages 78, 131, 146), David Roberts, and Sir John Steell (page 134) were all pupils there. Most were in some way connected with the Royal Scottish Academy: Sir William Allan (pages 123, 133, 135) was its second President, from 1837 to 1850; W. Borthwick Johnstone (page 147 and figure 29) was its Librarian from 1853 to 1857 and Treasurer from 1856 to 1868.

Hill's relatives were also, naturally, favourite subjects. With so many brothers and sisters he had plenty of nephews and nieces, and it seems that most of the children in the calotypes—often shown asleep, as in some of the photographs by Lewis Carroll, for that must have been about the only way to keep them still—were related to him in some way. The nephews and nieces themselves soon had children, and so there are, for instance, several young Finlays (see figure 28), the children of Hill's niece Mrs. Charles Finlay (page 227).

Hill's really close friends found themselves drawn into his passion for fancy dress and *tableaux vivants*. He seems to have been the producer of many such entertainments at fashionable parties (Lord Cockburn was especially fond of them) and he naturally tried to record some of his successes in photographs. There are several examples in Volume II of the National Portrait Gallery albums, and all involve members of the Edinburgh art world. "The Monks of Kennaquhair" (figure 29), inspired by Sir Walter Scott's novel *The Monastery*, for instance, includes David Scott, a prolific painter of historical and religious subjects; W. Borthwick Johnstone; and W. Leighton Leitch, who taught water-colour painting to Queen Victoria from about 1839 until Prince Albert's death in 1861. Leitch himself described how, after her first lesson, the Queen exclaimed: "This is very wonderful, and I am delighted; but I am surprised that I have never had this explained before." As Leitch continued these lessons at Windsor, Osborne, and Balmoral for twenty-two years, Victoria became quite proficient. Clarkson Stanfield, the marine and theatrical painter whom Leitch much admired, said of one of her paintings (not knowing that it was by the Queen): "Well, she paints too well for an amateur. She will soon be entering the ranks as a professional artist."[*]

The sculptor John Henning had just the kind of dignified old man's face to suit him for characters in *tableaux*, and there are three

[*]A. MacGeorge, *W. Leighton Leitch, Landscape Painter, A Memoir* (London, Blackie & Son, 1884).

27. James Ballantine—page 144; see also pages 140, 149, 151.

28. The Finlay children—page 283.

29. "The Monks of Kennaquhair"—page 292.

30. John Henning as Edie Ochiltree—
page 302; see also pages 301, 303.

pictures showing him as Edie Ochiltree, the "Gaberlunzie Man," in Sir Walter Scott's novel *The Antiquary*. As Lord Cockburn's daughter appears in two of these as the novel's Miss Wardour, they were presumably taken at Bonaly Tower. Other *tableaux* were taken at Merchiston Castle Academy, where John Gibson taught and was, in 1850, to become headmaster, with the boys as actors, but no sample is in the National Portrait Gallery albums. One wonders whether Hill had any thought of turning photography to the purposes of his earlier work in book illustration. Hugh Miller predicted, in the article from *The Witness* already mentioned, that there would be "in the probability, a new mode of design for the purposes of the engraver, especially for all the illustrations of books," and the writer John Gibson Lockhart wrote to Professor John Wilson: "This art is about to revolutionise book-illustration entirely."*

In some instances, what may seem to be merely a taste for fancy dress had some justification. The pictures of the Irish harper Patrick Byrne, dressed as an Ossianic bard, or perhaps to illustrate Scott's *Lay of the Last Minstrel* (see figure 31), may not have been entirely inappropriate to the kind of music he played, and the photographs of "Mr. Lane" in Indian and African costumes (pages 298, 299, 300) may have had similar rationales. "Mr. Lane" is usually identified as Edward William Lane, eminent Arabic and Egyptian scholar and translator, but there is no evidence that he visited Britain during the years when Hill and Adamson were photographing, nor do other pictures of him resemble those taken by Hill and Adamson.

Most interesting of all in this group are the pictures Hill called "Kahkewaquonaby, a Canadian Chief" (pages 289, 290) and "The Waving Plume" (figure 32). These have at various times been called "the first photographs ever taken of a Red Indian" and "photographs of a Welsh missionary to Canada, the Reverend Peter Jones." The truth, intriguingly, is a mixture of both descriptions.

The Reverend Peter Jones (1802–56) was born in Burlington Heights, near the western end of Lake Ontario. His father was a white man of Welsh descent, Augustus Jones, a government surveyor, and his mother, Tuhbenahneeguay, a Missisauga Indian on the New Credit Reserve, Brantford, Ontario. Jones spent his childhood with the tribe as an Indian and was given the name "Kahkewaquonaby," or, literally, "Sacred Waving Eagle's Plume" (or "Feathers")—hence Hill's "The Waving Plume." When Peter Jones was sixteen his father

31. Patrick Byrne as an Ossianic bard—
page 294; see also pages 293, 295, 296.

32. "The Waving Plume"—page 291.

*Quoted in Francis Caird Inglis, "D.O. Hill R.S.A. and His Work," *Journal of Edinburgh Photographic Society*, volume XIX, no. 258, June 1909, pp. 75ff.

took him away from the tribe and he was baptised in the Wesleyan Methodist Church. At the age of twenty-five, he went on his first tour as a missionary to the Indians. He became a deacon of the Church in 1830, a priest in 1833, and devoted the rest of his life to missionary work among the Missisauga, Munsee, Chippewa, and Iroquois tribes, by all of whom he seems to have been held in high esteem. He was later adopted as a Grand River Mohawk.

Jones visited Britain at least four times. On the third trip, October 1844 to April 1845, he gave a number of lectures which were particularly popular in Scotland. After one of these he and his wife "breakfasted with the great Dr. Chalmers,"* and it was presumably about this time that the Hill and Adamson calotypes were taken.

Though Hill and Adamson took Jones in European dress as well, the three pictures in the National Portrait Gallery albums show him as an Indian chief, and the metal peace pipe which he carries is very similar to that shown in a lithograph in Jones's book *History of the Ojebway Indians.* Jones himself wrote of "the beautiful pipe tomahawk presented to Kahkewaquonaby (Rev. Peter Jones) in the year 1838 by Colonel Sir Augustus d'Este [sic], son of the late Duke of Sussex, and used at a 'general Council' at the Credit Mission, Upper Canada, in Jan. 1840."† It appears that the Hill and Adamson calotypes are indeed the oldest known surviving photographs of a North American Indian. The nearest rivals are a score of daguerreotypes (including three famous ones of Keokuk) taken about 1846 or 1847 by Thomas M. Easterly and now mostly in the collection of the Missouri Historical Society, St. Louis.

Hill and Adamson also took the first known photograph of a Highland chief, that of George Gunn, factor to the Duke of Sutherland and chief of the Gunn clan of Caithness and Sutherland (figure 33). It is a pity that more of Hill and Adamson's portraits cannot have been of such fascinating and exotic characters, instead of so many ministers of the Free Church. The portraits of the latter, however, were greatly appreciated almost as soon as they were first known. One of the earliest reviews of them, that of an exhibition early in 1844 at "Mr. Gibson's, St. Catherine Street, Cupar," comments:

> Many of the portraits are not only likenesses but faithful representations of real life; they not only recall to the mind the indi-

33. *George Gunn—page 212.*

*Rev. Peter Jones, *Life and Journals of Kahkewaquonaby* (Anson Green, Toronto, 1860).
†Rev. Peter Jones, *History of the Ojebway Indians; with Especial Reference to their Conversion to Christianity* (A. W. Bennett, London, 1861).

34. David Maitland McGill Crichton—page 93.

viduals whose portraits they are, but the observer cannot help feeling that he is in the presence of the living, acting original. We would especially remark this as the effect of Mr. M. M. Crichton in a single portrait; Dr. Cunningham's in a group of three . . .*

David Maitland McGill Crichton of Rankeillour (figure 34), lay leader of the Disruptionists, Fife landowner, and free trader, was photographed for inclusion in the Disruption painting.

•

A final group of portraits is the very well-known series of about seventy photographs (thirty-seven are in the National Portrait Gallery albums) taken in the fishing village of Newhaven, on the Firth of Forth, a mere two miles from Princes Street and Rock House. James Fairbairn, minister there since January 1838, took part in the Disruption in 1843 and perhaps met Hill and Adamson when they photographed him for the memorial painting. If so, it seems plausible that he enlisted their help in his campaign to replace the dangerous and uncomfortable open fishing boats then in use and that these photographs were originally taken for fund-raising purposes. Certainly Fairbairn (seen in the calotype on page 179, which actually seems to have been posed outside Rock House rather than in Newhaven itself) got together over £15,000, enough to build or convert thirty-three properly decked boats and buy new fishing tackle for them. One negative from this series is dated June 1845, and the whole set was probably taken at about this time.

The unique and characteristic costume of the Newhaven fishwives, described fully in Roy Strong's essay, originated from the fact that the Newhaven community was founded by Huguenot immigrants who settled along the Firth of Forth (some of the older inhabitants still use the French *mère* for "mother"). The girls were familiar sights in the Edinburgh streets, carrying their baskets, or creels, and crying their wares of "caller cod" (fresh cod), "herrin," and "ow-oo" (oysters), "new drawn frae the Forth." James Nasmyth (figure 38), in his autobiography, remembers the oysters costing two shillings sixpence per hundred. But the fishwives were also known for other reasons. Within years of Hill and Adamson's picturesque photographs, *The Scotsman* was complaining that the costume

35. Fisher Lassies—page 178.

---

* *Fife Herald and Kinross, Strathearn and Clackmannan Advertiser*, January 25th, 1844.

served to identify women who were always to be found loitering in "shebeens" and brothels and suggesting that their morals left something to be desired. Soon even the freshness of their fish was being questioned, and one reads of the girls arriving at Waverley Station by train, unloading their creels from the luggage van, and buying fish from the city fishmongers for resale. Today Newhaven has lost all its charm and seems just a continuation of Leith and its docks, but Hill and Adamson's pictures of the fishermen and their boats, of the fishwives and boys, of the narrow cobbled streets and the grey stone houses are still—as Sir David Brewster found them—amongst the most immediately attractive of their work and, though scarcely examples of "reportage" or "photo-journalism" in the modern sense, are some of the earliest photographs to document ordinary working people in their ordinary costume and environment. A few similar pictures are amongst those taken of Adamson's home town and issued as *A Series of Calotype Views of St. Andrews Published by D. O. Hill and R. Adamson at their Calotype Studio, Calton Stairs, Edinburgh, 1846.* The twenty-one full-page illustrations and one small vignette were, of course, not reproduced by any printing process, but separate photographic copies of each calotype were made for each copy of the album.

36. Fishermen at Home—page 158.

The Albums

The most common size of Hill and Adamson's pictures was about $8^{11}/_{16} \times 6^{1}/_{2}$ inches (220 × 165 millimeters), the dimensions which came to be known as "full plate." But they used at least three other sizes of camera, the smallest taking pictures of roughly 5 × 4 inches (125 × 100 millimeters) and the larger taking pictures measuring 12 × 10 inches (305 × 255 millimeters) and $16^{1}/_{8} \times 12$ inches (410 × 305 millimeters). In the album of calotypes (now in the London Library) which Hill presented to Lord Cockburn after Adamson's death, he wrote: "This size [$16^{1}/_{8} \times 12$ inches] of calotype is, so far as I know, the largest yet made. Along with others of a similar size, it was executed in [1846 or 7?] by Robert Adamson, with a camera made by Davidson of Edinburgh." Davidson himself later wrote that the camera was "about two feet square, fitted up for taking portraits as large as life. But the imperfections in it, and the difficulty of preparing paper so large were against it."* So, too, as far as

*In his letter to the *Liverpool and Manchester Photographic Journal*, October 1859.

portraits were concerned, must have been the increased exposure time, and none of the five examples of this huge negative and print size in the albums is a portrait (see pages 251, 252–3, 330–1, 332–3, 334–5), though "Two Fisherwomen" (page 186) is large enough to be perhaps a portion of such a photograph.

After they had been working for a year or two, Hill and Adamson began to bind sets of their calotypes into imperial folio albums. For one thing, this was obviously a good way to assemble the pictures for presentation or sale and the going price was between £40 and £50,* which, allowing for the value of the pound in those days, makes the prices currently commanded by their prints not quite so inflated as they at first seem. But the albums were also surely intended to help solve the problem of which all calotypists were increasingly aware: fading of the prints. Fox Talbot himself was much attacked for this, especially as regards the calotypes that were included with the issue of the *Art Union* magazine in June 1846. The work of his first licensee, the miniature painter Henry Collen, who started taking calotypes in August 1841 and whose processing was done at Fox Talbot's Reading establishment, has survived today only in the overpainting which he used to make his "photographic sketches"; the basic photographic images themselves have virtually disappeared. But many writers commented on the dark and rich colours of the original calotypes and these must have had something like the deep brown, slightly purplish hue which one sees in those few albums which have been shut away from the light for a substantial part of the century and a quarter since they were taken. In fact, Adamson's calotypes have faded less than almost anyone else's—a tribute to his chemical skill.

There are three kinds of albums in existence: books of loose calotypes (which were from the very beginning on sale at the Princes Street shop of Hill's brother Alexander and which were sold at the Great Exhibition for five shillings each), made up by those who bought or obtained individual copies; the albums put together by Hill and Adamson themselves for sale; and the presentation albums. These last are naturally the most elaborate and carefully prepared, and Hill had very precise ideas on how they should be assembled,

*The North British Review, No. XIV, August 1847, pp. 465–504, refers to "the large volumes of Talbotypes published by *Messrs. Adamson and Hill* at the price of £40 or £50 each and now in the possession of one or two of the most distinguished artists in London."

as he wrote to John Scott, an Edinburgh man who had gone to London to work for P. & D. Colnaghi & Co., Ltd., the famous art dealers and print sellers. Hill tried to persuade him to bind and sell albums of the work Hill had by then ceased to produce but from which he hoped to continue to make an income:

> I have been very long in fulfilling the promise I volunteered when in London of sending you some specimens of the Calotypes I made in conjunction with my lamented friend Mr. Robert Adamson. I have now the pleasure of sending you a hundred (pray gratify me by accepting of them) & have selected them with some care in the hope that you may be induced to mount & bind them in a way similar to that in which Eastlake's and [Stanfield's] are got up.*

The album which Hill presented in 1845 to Clarkson Stanfield is now in the Gernsheim Collection, and Stanfield said of it: "I sat up till nearly three o'clock looking over them. They are indeed most wonderful and I would rather have a set of them than the finest Rembrandts I ever saw." The album given to Sir Charles Eastlake is probably the one now in the Victoria and Albert Museum, London. A similar album, "presented to the Right Honourable James Wilson on his departure for India," is in the British Museum.

Hill's letter to Scott goes on:

> Let me shortly describe these. The Calotypes are mounted on half colombier stone plate paper—this is done by a copperplate printer in the same way that indice proofs are printed. . . . In binding them up I have adopted a somewhat extravagant style of binding—morocco gilt edge—each leaf mounted on a guard of satin ribbon for strength as well as appearance—between the leaves a leaf of thin glazed paper—as tissue paper. The binding of each of our volumes cost about 5 guineas . . . on the title page—one of the calotypes should be used as a vignette. This may be the Greyfriars Tomb—with the artist sitting sketching & the girls looking on and the lettering thus done in faint sepia or gold liquid with a hair pencil.

* Hill to John Scott, October 25th, 1848, in the Edinburgh Room, Central Public Library, Edinburgh.

At this point Hill has drawn small sketches of the frontispiece, with the title "One Hundred Pictures in CALOTYPE BY D. O. HILL R.S.A. AND R. ADAMSON, Edinburgh MDCCCXLVIII," and the spine, showing how the "back title" should be printed.

Hill specifies exactly how photographs of Adamson and himself should be used: "The portrait of my amiable friend Adamson—who did much for the art—cut to a smallish oval—might be on a preliminary title.—I forget what binders call it, thus." Here there is another quick sketch. "My own large portrait might be opposite to his—or opposite the larger title page." In the National Portrait Gallery albums, portraits of Hill are used as frontispieces to Volumes I and II, and one of Adamson to Volume III. The requisite picture of Greyfriars Churchyard (Sir Robert Dennistoun's tomb) with Hill and two girls (his nieces the Misses Morris) appears on the title page of Volume I.

Hill asks Scott to "Pray excuse all this minuteness on a subject you may consider very unworthy of it—although 'tis one on which I feel somewhat warmly. I would like they should appear in their best attire in taking up their residence with you. . . ." The excuse for repeating much of his letter here is that it exactly describes the three National Portrait Gallery albums. His dedication is reproduced on page 71 of this book.

The calotypes were mounted by Colnaghi's exactly as Hill specified, one to a page on heavy card, bound into three 24 × 19-inch albums. The card is cream-coloured, and Hill says of the colour to be used: "An artist . . . tells me he finds mounting the Calotypes on faintly tinted Crayon papers gives a nature to the light which they do not possess on white paper. But follow your own luck in this matter." These albums, completed in 1848, were collectively titled *Calotype Studies by D. O. Hill, R.S.A. and Robert Adamson* and dated "Edinburgh 1843–1848." Volume I contained *Portraits* (one hundred two photographs); Volume II, *Portraits, Groups. &c &c.* (seventy-eight photographs); and Volume III, *Newhaven Fishermen. Landscapes. Buildings. &. &.* (seventy-eight photographs). The bindings now seem a little heavy and over-elaborate for the pictures which were mounted in them, and they are certainly not of especially good quality. Although they do not seem to have been much used in their years at the Royal Academy, the albums had to be rebacked sometime early in the present century, and when they arrived at the National Portrait Gallery the leather was drying out and many of the pages were coming away from the binding. Restoration work was done on the albums at the British Museum and red dye was found to have been applied to the leather covers, perhaps to make them match the new spines.

With a few exceptions, all the calotypes in the National Portrait Gallery albums are captioned in pencil in Hill's own minuscule writing. In his letter to Scott, he said: "I have written the names in pencil on all the subjects—they might be, if you cared for it, printed in faint sepia letters on the mounting paper, under each picture." This last stage never took place, which is perhaps as well, since Hill's own captions might have been erased; despite his occasional blanks and errors, his own titles to the pictures are an invaluable source of information and in some cases have solved riddles about the identity of people and places which have been unanswerable for years. Wherever possible (and legible), it is Hill's captions which have been used in this book, though they have been amplified and corrected in most cases.

There is one other aspect of Hill's instructions in his letter: "The white spots must be carefully stippled out—with watercolours of the same tint." As far as can be seen, no retouching has been done on the prints in the National Portrait Gallery albums (though many of the *negatives* have certainly been retouched, as already explained), but it is of course possible that it was so skilfully done as to be now unidentifiable, though this seems doubtful.

The End of the Partnership

The pressure of work kept up by the extrovert, energetic Hill during his four and a half years of photography at Rock House was at last too much for the always unhealthy Adamson. Late in 1847 Adamson retired to convalesce at the family home in St. Andrews, and on January 14th, 1848, he died, aged only twenty-seven. This gives yet more significance to the albums prepared in 1848, and they become in a real sense a memorial to his vital role in the partnership, for with Adamson's technical skill and chemical knowledge gone, Hill could not solve the increasingly troubling problem of fading, and he soon gave up photography in favour of a return to painting. The album which Hill presented to Lord Cockburn in August 1850 has a caption to a picture of Dr. John Adamson in Hill's handwriting which states: "His brother Robert during the last five years of his life devoted himself, with my aid as an artist, in developing the process of the art. The pictures in this volume are chiefly manufactured by him and are his last monument."

John Adamson, whom Hill called in the same caption "one of the earliest and most skilful improvers of the Calotype," nearly came back into the story at this point, for there appears to have been some discussion of his taking over Robert's share of the enterprise. Adamson must have felt that he should benefit from Robert's legacy of work: Hill notes, in a letter written on August 21st, 1848, to Samuel Carter Hall, editor of the *Art Union*, in which a number of Hill and Adamson calotypes were published, that "the settlement of my calotype affairs" was "pending between me & the friends of my late friend and partner . . . Robert Adamson." Obviously, Hill had wanted either to get the sole right to exploit the calotypes or to sell this to the Adamson family, and he had hoped to write to Hall "either as the sole proprietor of the Calotypes—or as having given up my interest in them altogether." The politeness of his letter scarcely conceals his annoyance at "having come a distance of 100 miles solely to get this calotype affair of ours settled," only to find no one from the Adamson family present, so that he "must speak for Mr. Adamson's relations who with myself have been put to heavy expenses by these Calotype labours."

But John Adamson's medical practice had improved dramatically and he decided not to join Hill. Whatever arrangement, if any, was worked out between them, Hill seems to have temporarily abandoned everything to do with photography (except for his sporadic attempts to make money out of the surviving calotypes) in the autumn of 1848 and to have become more and more involved in his landscapes and in the work of the Royal Scottish Academy. He also helped found the Scottish National Gallery and the Association for the Promotion of the Fine Arts in Scotland, a fund to buy contemporary work which was largely financed by a lottery. He met John Ruskin and promoted the career of Noël Paton (1821–1901), friend of Sir John Millais's and prolific painter of mainly religious subjects, who later became Sir Joseph Noël Paton and succeeded Sir William Allan as Queen's Limner for Scotland.

In 1858, though he had taken no photographs for a decade, Hill became a council member of the Photographic Society of Scotland (founded, with Sir David Brewster as its first President, in April 1856), but had left it by the time it was discontinued in 1867. Between 1860 and 1862 he dabbled in photography again, collaborating with the Glasgow photographer A. M'Glashon on *Some Contributions towards the Further Development of Fine Art in Photography*, an album of fourteen pictures published in 1862. These photographs, "designed and arranged" by Hill and photographed by M'Glashon using the collodion process, are weak and conventional, but this is scarcely surprising. The calotypes made with Adamson came at the brief moment in history when photography had not had time to get into the hands of professional operators and when the time and effort that had to be put into each picture by the pioneers of the process created individual and uniquely forceful images. Hill's artistic taste (as clearly shown in Roy Strong's essay) had always been conventional, and once this was applied to a technique that had become all too easy, it could hardly fail to produce slick and shallow pictures. Surely, too, Adamson was not the mere technical assistant he is usually made out to be.

In 1861 Hill's daughter, Charlotte, married Walter Scott Dalgleish, and in 1862 Hill took a second wife, Amelia Paton, the sculptress sister of Noël. "She will make me finish the picture," he wrote to his sister-in-law in Perth. The picture he meant was the long-awaited Disruption painting, and he was right about Amelia making him finish it. Although he had exhibited nothing in the Royal Scottish Academy's exhibition in 1861, and one might suppose that his energy had at last begun to flag, he returned to the painting with a will. It was finally ready to show the world in 1866.

The First General Assembly of the Free Church of Scotland,
Signing the Act of Separation and Deed of Demission,
at Tanfield, Edinburgh, May, 1843

It needs a painting five feet high and eleven feet four inches long to justify such a title, and when it is blazoned in letters over an inch high along the bottom of the painting, it needs every bit of that eleven feet four inches. But size is no measure of quality, and the inescapable fact is that the Disruption painting, as one must go on calling it, is a monumental flop. Despite its vast size, far too much is crammed into too little space, for Hill was the victim of his own ambition and the Free Church's success. He might have done better had he not accepted advice to change the subject. The original Deed of Demission was signed by one hundred fifty-five ministers and this sort of number could be effectively composed in a painting, as demonstrated by Hayter's *Trial of Queen Caroline* or David's *Coronation of Napoleon.*

But Hill determined to depict in his painting all the ministers who finally signed the Deed of Demission. Indeed, he went further and included a number of people who were not present but who, because of their sympathies with the Church, he felt *ought* to have been. So, for instance, Adamson (in the pose on page 229) is shown with a camera, Henning and Alexander Handyside Ritchie (page 78) are shown with a Newhaven man and woman looking through the left-hand skylight, and the Reverend J. Julius Wood (figure 37) is included, although he was too ill to travel from Malta in time for the first General Assembly, so his wife stood in for him. The offer for sale of the photographs admitted this in referring to Dr. Alexander Duff, of the Bengal Mission: "This is by no means the only anachronism in the Picture; these, and it is hoped the apologies for their occurrence, will scarcely require to be more specially adverted to."

Hill's motives for these additions are not entirely clear: to an extent, he obviously wanted to make his painting as grand as possible and to leave virtually no space unfilled by a face. Partly he may have wished to honour—or flatter—his friends and colleagues. John Miller, for instance, the railway engineer who commissioned so many paintings from Hill, is given a prominent place. But one cannot escape the feeling that, since he wanted to sell the picture itself for as much as he could, and as many photographic copies as possible, he saw a sheer commercial advantage in including everyone he could think of:

> It has been the ambition and aim of the Painter, to render his representation of the Disruption Assembly a desirable, if not indispensable, heirloom in the homes of all Free Churchmen . . . he has been careful to exclude from his canvas any episodical passage or incident which might by possibility have given offence to any individual or Church [and he] entertains the hope, therefore, that the representation . . . will find ready admission into the houses and Art Collections of men of all denominations of religious opinions, both in our own and other lands.*

37. The Reverend J. Julius Wood—page 81.

*The Disruption of the Church of Scotland: An Historical Picture . . .

Such a motive would certainly explain Hill's curious decision to alter in the painting the faces of some of those who were still alive when it was at last completed. Dr. George Bell (page 91) and the Reverend D. T. K. Drummond (page 80), for instance, have had grey whiskers added to age them appropriately, but what other justification can there be for this unhistoric and anachronistic alteration of some of the participants in the Disruption and not others?

Hill's strategy—if strategy it was—did not altogether come off. The painting had mainly favourable reviews in all the Scottish newspapers, quotations from which take up nineteen pages in the offer for sale of the photographs. The *Caledonian Mercury* (May 24th, 1866) called it "a great and enduring work of art" and the *Greenock Daily Telegraph* (January 15th, 1867) said: "It is more than a success—it is a triumph." *The Scotsman* (June 1st, 1864) trumpeted: "Surely there is but one place for this picture, and that is the National Gallery," and two years later (May 24th, 1866) the same newspaper thought it better than Hayter's *The Great Reform Bill, 1832.*[*] But many of the reviewers also referred to the drabness of the Tanfield Hall setting and the Free Church ministers' attire, and the dullness of the almost symmetrical composition chosen by Hill. Hayter's painting is open to the same criticisms, but Hill's Scottish ministers could not even be shown in the bright red waistcoats sported by most of Hayter's Members of Parliament, and the resulting drabness, together with the twenty-three-year delay in showing the painting, lessened its appeal and impact. Hill had set a price of £3,000 on it, but though the Free Church exhibited it widely to raise the sum by appeal (at the Calton Convening Rooms, Edinburgh, and the McClure Galleries, Glasgow, in 1866, and in Aberdeen in 1867), they received only £1,200 and, in the end, Hill accepted £1,500. It was hung in the Free Church offices on The Mound, Edinburgh, where it can still be seen.

The photographs of the painting, made while the finishing touches were still being applied, are in a way more interesting. To quote the offer for sale again:

> ... the Portraits [were] made, chiefly for this Picture, in 1843 by Mr. Hill and his late friend, Mr. Robert Adamson of St. Andrews, by the then newly-discovered Photographic Process of Mr. Fox Talbot, called the Calotype or Talbotype,—until

[*] Which the government had purchased for the National Portrait Gallery, London, in 1858.

then almost unknown or unapplied as a vehicle of artistic thought and expression, ... it is a striking coincidence that, while the commencement of the Picture was thus marked by the elevation and higher application of Photography, its completion seems destined, by a combination of improved processes, to aid in the inauguration of a new era in the reproduction of Works of Art.

This refers to the fact that Thomas Annan (1828–87), a photographer from Glasgow, had had a special camera made by John Henry Dallmeyer, the celebrated German lens maker who came to London in 1851, to photograph such a large object. The carbon printing process newly patented by Joseph Swan of Newcastle[*] was used to make prints, and these were sold in three sizes, 24 × 9 inches (sold at one and a half guineas), 32 × 14 inches (sold at four guineas), and 48 × 21¼ inches, actually made up of three overlapping sections (sold at eight guineas). "Selected artist's proof" copies of each photograph cost half as much again as an ordinary print and, between all the various alternatives, some four hundred prints were subscribed for.[†]

It is all very ironic, for Hill himself surely only regarded photography as a means to an end and would have expected to be remembered for his painting rather than for any connection with the new art. Heinrich Schwarz, author of the first serious twentieth-century assessment of the Hill and Adamson calotypes, wrote: "Hill's noblest work proceeded from the need and served the need of his paltriest. He squandered his inspired camera portraits ... on a sort of 'frozen photomontage.' "[‡]

James Nasmyth (figure 38), who spent much time with Hill in Edinburgh and Bonaly, wrote in his autobiography of his "dear departed friend":

38. James Nasmyth—page 208.

[*]This, later known as the "Autotype" process, was the subject of Swan's first patent, Patent No. 503, 1864. In 1902 the Royal Photographic Society awarded him its progress medal for the invention.
[†]Dr. J. R. Fleming, in his already-quoted description of the first Free Assembly's "vivid appeal to the people at large," goes on to say: "Of this the picture by D. O. Hill, which in its engraved form found way into thousands of Scottish households, is a permanent memento. Not only does it graphically represent the signing of the 'Act of Separation and Deed of Demission' by ministers and elders of every degree: it conveys the impression of an applauding and deeply interested chorus of sympathisers" (A History of the Church in Scotland, 1843–1874).
[‡]David Octavius Hill, der Meister der Photographie (Leipzig, 1931), translated by Hélène E. Fraenkel as David Octavius Hill, Master of Photography (Harrap, London, 1932).

His name calls up many recollections of happy hours spent in his company. He was, in all respects, the incarnation of geniality. His lively sense of humour, combined with a romantic and poetic constitution of mind, and his fine sense of the beautiful in Nature and art, together with his kindly and genial feeling, made him, all in all, a most agreeable friend and companion. "D. O. Hill," as he was generally called . . . was a very frequent visitor at our Edinburgh fireside, and was ever ready to join in our extemporised walks and jaunts, when he would overflow with his kindly sympathy and humour. He was a skilful draughtsman, and possessed a truly poetic feeling for art. His designs for pictures were always attractive, from the fine feeling exhibited in their composition and arrangement. But somehow, when he came to handle the brush, the result was not always satisfactory—a defect not uncommon among artists. Altogether, he was a delightful companion and a staunch friend, and his death made a sad blank in the artistic society of Edinburgh.[*]

Three years after finishing the Disruption painting Hill became very ill with rheumatic fever and was forced to give up his post as secretary of the Royal Scottish Academy. He and Amelia moved from Rock House to a larger home (once a farm) at Newington Lodge, Mayfield Terrace, and on May 17th, 1870, he died. His entire photographic stock was valued at £70 and most of his obituaries did not even mention his collaboration with Adamson. The exception was *The Scotsman* for May 18th: ". . . the partners produced a series of pictures known as Calotypes which to this day stand unsurpassed as specimens of truly artistic photography." But otherwise it was an episode which Hill—and the public—had forgotten.

It was some twenty-five years before the tide began to turn again. Three men began to make new prints of the calotypes and to encourage a widespread appreciation of their artistic value. Most important was Andrew Elliott, one of Hill's many nephews, who took over Alexander Hill's print shop and its stock of calotype positives. His book *Calotypes* has already been quoted, and he and his son had many carbon prints made by Jessie Bertram, a first-class technician who, from 1913 to 1925, made perhaps the best—and certainly the most permanent—of the copies produced in the twentieth century. Francis Caird Inglis, who bought Rock House soon after 1900 (it

[*] *James Nasmyth, Engineer, an Autobiography,* edited by Samuel Smiles (John Murray, London, 1883).

had continued to be a photographic studio, and there is an 1874 photograph of it showing that the occupant then was an "Archibald Burns, Photographer"), found many negatives which Hill had not even bothered to take with him when he moved out in 1869. From them Inglis made glass negatives and carbon prints. J. Craig Annan, who as a child had known Hill through his father, Thomas Annan, also made prints from the original negatives.

Important Hill and Adamson exhibitions contributed to the revival of interest in their work: there was one at the Royal Photographic Society, London, in 1898, and one at the Seventh International Exhibition of the Art of Photography in Hamburg a year later. In 1930 the *Illustrated London News* referred to Hill as "the Old Master of Photography" and "the Raeburn of the Camera," and Schwarz's important book—written, significantly, by a man who had had training in art, worked at the Albertina in Vienna, and was Assistant Curator of the Austrian State Gallery at the Belvedere in Vienna—was published soon after. The pioneering contribution of Helmut Gernsheim has already been mentioned, and, in 1970, an influential Scottish Arts Council exhibition, commemorating the centenary of Hill's death, was organized by Katherine Michaelson of Edinburgh, who wrote a full and detailed catalogue. These last three experts have played the greatest roles in the rediscovery of calotypes, and all—in person or through their writing—have been of inestimable help to me in preparing this book. If I have any disagreement with them, it is that all usually stress Hill's importance at the expense of Adamson's—but, to be fair, so little is known of the younger man and his life that it is difficult to write about him.

Hill and Adamson's superb calotype results were never equalled, and even when the process had been overtaken by better ones, only the Frenchman "Nadar" (Gaspard Félix Tournachon, 1820–1910) and the English amateur Julia Margaret Cameron (1815–79) approached their skill as portraitists.

"Those wonderful relics of the earliest days of photography which remain the most consummate masterpieces it has ever produced," wrote Schwarz of David Octavius Hill, calling him "Master of Photography." Add the name of Robert Adamson as another "Master" and one can only agree. The album pages are full of the best portraits taken by the best portraitists of the nineteenth century.

D.O. HILL AND THE

ACADEMIC TRADITION

ROY STRONG

39. David Octavius Hill—page 224—from Volume II of the albums.

David Octavius Hill was forty when he began his momentous collaboration with a young man twenty years his junior, Robert Adamson. By 1843, the year in which the studio at Rock House, on Calton Hill, in Edinburgh opened, Hill had been secretary of the newly founded Royal Scottish Academy for thirteen years and enjoyed a reputation both as a landscape painter and as an illustrator of some talent, besides being an accomplished figure in Edinburgh society. The National Portrait Gallery albums are a very personal expression of the minds and talents of these two remarkable men and in particular of Hill, who presented them to the Royal Academy of Arts in London that they might remain for posterity as a monument to his creative work in a new art form, the photograph. The albums consist of three folio volumes, each of which opens with an initial visual statement about the men themselves, Hill in the first two and Adamson in the third. These "self-portraits" define the characters of the two men very precisely. Hill prefaces Volume I, elegantly leaning against a masonry wall, his left hand fingering his waistcoat buttons, his right at his side holding a top hat (page 223). There is an element of chic, and a buttonhole sprouts from his lapel. Volume II records him in his role as the heroic artist, posed in profile, his cloak swagged around him, echoing in a new medium a formula derived from classical antiquity (figure 39). Adamson opens the last of the volumes. In contrast to Hill, he is pensive, his eyes downcast, seated with one arm resting upon a table piled with books (figure 40). These opening images sum up the nature of the relationship: Hill, theatrical in manner, extrovert in behaviour, a man preoccupied with surface appearances; Adamson, introvert, composed,

40. Robert Adamson—page 230—from Volume III of the albums.

contained, and controlled. Together these characteristics formed the delicate balance which found its supreme expression in the two hundred fifty-eight calotypes in the National Portrait Gallery albums.

Essentially they will forever remain the technical achievement of Robert Adamson, always the most shadowy figure, but, one would deduce, the man who possessed that ultra-sensitivity to character and atmosphere missing from the more prosaic Hill. Ironically, it was Hill who governed the visual repertory of the calotypes. He it was who posed the sitters, dictated their gestures, assembled and placed the props of table and chair, books and flowers, papers, as well as the more unusual impedimenta such as busts and casts from the Elgin Marbles. Although the expression of a moment in time, the poses were devised by a man whose visual imagination had been formed some twenty years before—in the 1820's. It is, in fact, accidental that Hill created anything new in his calotypes, for it is impossible to argue that he was anything more than an artist working within a tradition of picture-making created at the close of the eighteenth century and the opening of the nineteenth, a tradition which found its quintessential expression in the establishment in 1829 of what became the Royal Scottish Academy, of which Hill was secretary for almost forty years. It is ironic that the year in which Adamson tragically died, and in which the studio ceased to operate, was the year in which the Pre-Raphaelite Brotherhood came into being, in defiance of the type of art the academies represented.

Thus the calotypes of Hill and Adamson, considered strictly on an iconographical basis, transferred, as one would expect, to the new mechanical medium of the camera the visual repertory of almost any exhibition of the Royal Scottish Academy during the 1840's. Apart from the portrait photographs, which make up the bulk of the albums, the contents fall into three broad categories: thirty-seven pictures of fisherfolk at Newhaven; twenty-four titled genre compositions; and thirty-eight topographical views. (An odd one out, which anticipates the revolution which was to happen in the study of the art of the past, is the photograph of William Etty's painting *The Dance* [figure 41], exhibited at the Royal Academy and at the Birmingham Society of Artists in 1842, and now in a private collection). All these four groups, however, belong to established art forms inherited from the previous century. It is therefore necessary to our appreciation of Hill's calotypes—which James Caw, the historian of Scottish art, once described as "among the triumphs of photog-

41. Hill's calotype of William Etty's painting The Dance—*page 153.*

raphy" because they attained "effects so beautiful that they are still the envy and despair of the best photographers"—to approach them through their antecedents in Scottish academic painting of the early nineteenth century.

•

The portraits can be usefully subdivided into those of a single sitter, either male or female, those of groups, and those which are studies for Hill's Disruption painting. In the first category the portraits of single male sitters are united by a similar dramatic use of chiaroscuro effect. In every instance the head and hands are brilliantly set to catch the light, while the props of chair and documents, book and curtain, recede into a background of almost even tonality. This stylistic trick invests the portraits with a powerful and dramatic quality. Time and again one is drawn to study the reality of a human face, and the eye is not distracted by any other features within the area of the calotype. Partly, it must be said, this was the result of the technical limitations of the process, for which the sitter had to be posed in direct sunlight, but that this was a controllable effect we can deduce from the evidence of the female sitters, who were deliberately lit with even, arcadian sunshine. Somehow Hill and Adamson were trying to achieve, by careful arrangement and set-dressing, a certain effect. All artists tend to be inspired more by what they see of the work of their predecessors and contemporaries than by their own direct experience, and this is particularly so of a derivative minor painter such as Hill.

The portrait photographs, therefore, belong to a definite stylistic tradition of portrait painting in Scotland. In many ways, much of what has been described as their "enigmatic charm" springs from the fact that these photographs represent the final flowering of a concept of recording human likeness first established as a style by Sir Henry Raeburn at the close of the eighteenth century. Writing in 1908, James Caw could still look back and recognize the opening decades of the nineteenth century in Scotland as having produced a particular idiom in the portrait, a means of interpreting and presenting the sitter independent of those painters who dominated the south, the grand figures of Reynolds and Gainsborough, Romney and Lawrence. This difference may be summed up in the words "directness" and "expressiveness" applied to the portrayal of charac-

42. Thomas Duncan—page 124.

43. Sir Henry Raeburn: John Crichton Stuart, Second Marquess of Bute, 1821 (Marquess of Bute).

ter which was indigenous to Scottish art and found fulfilment in the work of Raeburn and his followers. They gave, Caw wrote:

> the portraiture of the earlier half of the last century a character of its own, and that distinctively Scottish. In this access of naturalism, with its greater dependence upon immediate impression of reality, and in the simplification of pictorial motive that involved, Raeburn played the most important part, and neither he nor Watson-Gordon, his most conspicuous successor, owed much to foreign schools.*

Thus the two key artists for the understanding of Hill and Adamson's male portraits are Sir Henry Raeburn (1756–1823) and Sir John Watson-Gordon (1788–1864).

Raeburn had been briefly taught by a minor portrait painter, David Martin, but later he visited Italy for a period of eighteen months. After his return to Edinburgh in 1787 he became the most fashionable portrait painter of the age, and remained so until his death, having been elected an Associate of the Royal Academy in London in 1814 and a Member in 1815 and knighted by George IV in 1822. All his portraits are distinguished by a dramatic chiaroscuro, in which strong light falls from the spectator's viewpoint onto the face and hands of the sitter. These he delineated in some detail, with forceful rectangular strokes of the brush, relegating the costume and background to the most summary of treatments. No modern scholar has studied in depth the portraiture of Raeburn, nor is anything known of his visit to Italy, so that one can only speculate as to the precise source of his highly idiosyncratic style. Somewhere, at some time, Raeburn must have seen portraits by Rembrandt; this preoccupation with the startling lighting of figures in portraits is a commonplace of his style. It is also a tradition which Raeburn could have picked up from Caravaggio and his followers. This formula the artist combined with a knowledge of the rapid bravura technique of a Frans Hals. Moreover, both Rembrandt and Hals embody a truth in the representation of their subjects that can be related to the honesty with which Raeburn observed his fellow countrymen. In this way he created a repertory of poses which were to be repeated by his followers until well into the nineteenth century.

In Scottish Painting, Past and Present (T. C. and E. C. Jack, Edinburgh and London, 1908).

44. Sir David Brewster—page 197.

45. Sir Henry Raeburn: Robert Caincart of Drum (Location unknown).

46. Sir Henry Raeburn: John Clerk, Lord Eldin (Scottish National Portrait Gallery).

47. *Sir John Watson-Gordon:* Right Honourable Charles Hope of Granton, *1832 (Major Hope Johnstone, Raehills).*

48. *Sir John Watson-Gordon:* Charlotte, Mrs. Hope, *1832 (Major Hope Johnstone, Raehills).*

49. *Mrs. Anna Brownell Jameson—page 219.*

Scottish portraiture thus paved the way for the camera's ruthless eye, for Raeburn, Watson-Gordon, and their followers were preparing people to accept the reality of themselves. Nearly any male portrait within the National Portrait Gallery albums can be parallelled with something by Raeburn. That of Thomas Duncan (figure 42) recalls the grandiloquent pose of Raeburn's *John Crichton Stuart, Second Marquess of Bute* (figure 43); Sir David Brewster (figure 44) can be compared with *Robert Caincart of Drum* (figure 45); the numerous portraits of men with books and papers can also be duplicated within the Raeburn repertory, *John Clerk, Lord Eldin* (figure 46), for example.

The style was inherited by Sir John Watson-Gordon, who succeeded Raeburn as the chief recorder of fashionable Scottish society in the 1830's and 1840's. Less brilliant than Raeburn, he was open to influences from the south, particularly that of the portraiture of Sir Thomas Lawrence, but he confessed also to a passionate admiration for the work of Velásquez. Watson-Gordon's portrait *Charles Hope of Granton*, signed and dated 1832 (figure 47), and that of Hope's wife, *Charlotte, Mrs. Hope* (figure 48), show the transmutation of the Raeburn formula, softened and made more slick by the tricks of painters of the post-Lawrence school. *Mrs. Hope* is not far off, however, from Hill's redoubtable Mrs. Jameson (figure 49), while the pose and presentation of *Charles Hope* can be parallelled many times within the albums (for example, figure 50). By the close of the 1830's and through the 1840's the style of Watson-Gordon's male portraits was to be the immediate inspiration for Hill's portrait arrangements. Hill was amply familiar with Watson-Gordon's work in his capacity as secretary of the Royal Scottish Academy, where Watson-Gordon regularly exhibited. Two portraits give an indication of the type of academic portraiture that Watson-Gordon was producing during the period of Hill and Adamson's collaboration: *Erskine Douglas Sandford* (figure 51), exhibited at the Royal Scottish Academy in 1839; and an undated example from the early 1840's, *Sir John Dalyell* (figure 52). Both are three-quarter length, with the typical trick of direct dramatic lighting of face and hands also characteristic of the photographs. They share, too, the same solemnity of mood.

Watson-Gordon was the most significant artist among a group which worked in this way and which included Andrew Geddes (1783–1844), Robert Scott Lauder (1803–69), and Colvin Smith

50. *Mr. Robert Bryson—page 357.*

51. *Sir John Watson-Gordon:* Erskine Douglas Sandford, *1839 (Faculty of Advocates, Edinburgh).*

52. *Sir John Watson-Gordon:* Sir John Dalyell *(Binns).*

(1795–1875). What we must visualize at the Rock House studio is this enormously calculated arrangement of props and lighting to make the calotype image approximate as closely as possible fashionable portraiture as practised in Scotland in the 1840's.

This applies to the men, but what of the women? Hill's visions of early Victorian womanhood stem from a source far different from that of Raeburn and his disciples. The photographs are not distinguished by extreme chiaroscuro effect so much as by a contrived prettiness. Miss Patricia Morris, in rustic attire, leans pensively against a balustrade entwined with flowers (figure 53); the Misses Binny and Miss Monro are posed like the Three Graces (figure 54), their arms lovingly entwined and arranged with trailing garland or shawl; Miss Murray delicately clasps her hand to her bosom as if to emphasize her charming profile (figure 55); Miss Elizabeth Rigby's skirts are arranged with the graceful severity of a portrait by Ingres (page 119). These are keepsake images calculated to evoke the quintessential ideal of female beauty in the 1840's: fragile and wilting, early Victorian, upper-class ladies with huge soulful eyes, upturned noses, dimpled cheeks, and tiny lips, long necks and small waists, forever deployed in poses of contemplative yet seductive resignation. These are manifestations in calotype form of a vast visual literature proliferating at every level of society during the 1830's and 1840's, but if one had to pick the classic handbook for these visions of ethereal, aristocratic loveliness it would be Heath's *Book of Beauty*, which appeared annually from 1833 to 1847. Each volume is illustrated with engravings of ladies of high rank in similar poses (figures 56, 57), often also adopting fancy-dress roles as the lady of romance, the gipsy, or the favourite of the sultan. Artistic licence enabled painters who contributed to the *Book of Beauty*, such as Alfred Chalon and Daniel Maclise, to achieve an idealization of their sitters which the camera could never succeed in doing. Indeed, one is struck most by the utter plainness of Hill's lady sitters—early Victorian ladies deprived of any cosmetic help—in spite of their efforts to achieve the contrary. And a glance through any of Heath's volumes for the 1840's reveals one of the traditions upon which Hill drew for nourishment in the composition of his female portraits. There is the same fashionable droop, the head and eyes downcast in resignation or turned despairingly upwards, a repertory of poses of contemplation or fashionable dalliance. Each time, Hill is deliberately composing his female sitters into a *tableau* in-

53. *Miss Patricia Morris—page 228.*

54. *The Misses Binny and Miss Monro—page 261.*

55. *Miss Murray—page 128.*

spired by those of the type created by artists for the *Book of Beauty*.

There is a third category of portraiture in the National Portrait Gallery albums which remains to be investigated, the group portrait. The majority of these are studies for Hill's vast *The First General Assembly of the Free Church of Scotland*, which falls within the tradition exemplified in Hill's own lifetime by the vast compositions of Benjamin Robert Haydon and Sir George Hayter, delineating in detail similar historic confrontations. Hill's project for this group, to commemorate the momentous event when nearly five hundred ministers left the Church of Scotland and established their own independent body, had first led him to use the calotype process as a short-cut for gathering together so many portraits. Far from accelerating the production of this work, it took Hill twenty-three years to produce what, at the most charitable, has been described as a "large and laborious picture."

The portraits within the albums evoke vividly the world in which Hill moved. They record Edinburgh intellectual and smart society in its silver age, that period after the death of Sir Walter Scott and before the erosion of local insularity by the spread of fast communications, which led to the increasing drift of talent south of the Border. With the exception of the Newhaven fisherfolk, Hill depicts Establishment society: clergymen, professors of the University of Edinburgh, lawyers and judges, fellow artists and members of the Royal Scottish Academy, the upper-class women who graced this milieu, and his own distinctly well-to-do relatives. Although the studies of clergymen reflect one of the most dramatic events of Scottish life in the 1840's, there is nothing else in the albums to indicate any of the realities of contemporary society, nothing to suggest the rapid urbanization and industrialization of Scotland, with its consequent exploitation of labour and appalling slum conditions. Hill lets his camera's eye dwell on the secure, closed, upper-class world in which he moved with such charming assurance. We catch glimpses of him at a house party at Bonaly Tower, the home of Lord Cockburn. He goes to dinner with John Murray, the publisher, where he meets the remarkable Elizabeth Rigby. In fact, the photographs drop names as much as those of any smart-society photographer of the present day. Much of their charm stems from Hill's ability to project a world (similar to that of Gainsborough's portraits) which we would like to inhabit, into which nothing unpleasant is ever allowed to encroach, in which the men are either handsome and debonair or

56. *Alfred Chalon:* The Lady Worsley (*Heath's* Book of Beauty, *1840*).

57. *Daniel Maclise:* The Misses Mary & Roma MacLeod of MacLeod (*Heath's* Book of Beauty, *1846*).

ruggedly grave and paternal, where women are young and winsome or old and kindly, where every child is instant enchantment, where working people are not sordid but picturesque, and where, at a moment's notice, everyone dons fancy dress and embarks on a *fête champêtre* in an Arcadia upon which the sun always shines.

•

The attitudes which govern the genre calotypes are not so very different from those governing the portraits. Before comment, it is worth listing the titles of most of these (the line between what is and what is not a genre subject is not always firmly drawn): "The Torso"; "Edinburgh Ale"; "A Discussion"; "The Monks of Kennaquhair"; "The House of Death"; "Irish Harper"; "Edie Ochiltree"; "The Morning after 'He Greatly Daring Dined' "; "Asleep"; "The Bedfellows"; "Sleeping Child"; "The Minnow Pool"; "Summer Noon"; "The Gowan"; "The Sleeping Flowergatherers"; "The Letter"; "Love Reverie"; "The Pastor's Visit"; "Cottage Door"; "Home from Market"; "Baiting the Line"; "Just Landed."

The subjects are all anecdotal and sentimental in theme. Some are inspired by episodes in the works of Scott and Burns (for example, figure 58) that relate directly to Hill's work as an illustrator. He contributed landscape views to the edition of the Waverley Novels brought out in 1831–32 by Robert Cadell (page 362), fourteen views to Allan Cunningham's edition of *The Works of Robert Burns*, and sixty-one to *The Land of Burns*, published in 1840 by John Blackie. He also illustrated the works of James Hogg, the Ettrick Shepherd. In the main, however, the calotypes belong to the unexplored world of Victorian genre painting. This type of subject matter was first popularized by the painter Sir David Wilkie, whose work drew on insular traditions—scenes of cottage life by George Morland or the eighteenth-century conversation piece—reinterpreted in the light of a study of seventeenth-century Dutch scenes of high and low life. The subject matter of Hill's genre calotypes is exactly what one would expect from a secretary of the Royal Scottish Academy familiar with the Wilkie tradition, especially as expressed by its leading contemporary exponent, Sir George Harvey. A selective listing of the titles of some of the paintings Harvey exhibited at the Academy during the period leading up to and including Hill and Adamson's collaboration is instructive:

58. John Henning and Miss Cockburn as characters in Sir Walter Scott's The Antiquary—*page 301; see also pages 302, 303.*

Other painters who exhibited genre pictures on similar themes at the Royal Scottish Academy during the 1840's include William Bonnar, who exhibited in 1841 *Edie Ochiltree in the Prison at Fairport* (compare pages 301, 303); John Graham Gilbert, who exhibited in 1850 *A Sleeping Girl* (compare pages 281, 285); and William Borthwick Johnstone (page 147), Hill's close friend and exhibitor of *Mother and Child Sleeping* (compare page 273).

This type of painting exactly parallels certain pictures in the National Portrait Gallery albums, although it does not explain the

59. Sir George Harvey: Quitting the Manse, *1848 (National Gallery of Scotland).*

60. William Etty: Guardian Cherubs: The Lady Mary and the Hon. Charles Agar, *1828 (Private Collection).*

61. Henry Weekes: Sleeping Child and Dog, *1851 (Illustrated Catalogue of the Great Exhibition, Volume II).*

motivation for such subjects. Undoubtedly, at the time they had a relevance which has since evaporated. Today we are merely left with a feeling of repugnance for most of the motifs. To take a single instance, the calotypes of children are often the kind which we now find the most offensive, with their almost sickening sentimentality. They represent a romantic view of childhood as a separate period of life, a concept unknown to the early eighteenth century, when children were dressed as miniature adults and encouraged to grow up as soon as possible in order to enjoy the privileges of the adult world and no particular value was attached to the charms of babyhood or to the innocence of childhood. The idea that the latter was somehow a particularly blessed state was essentially a romantic one and finds reflection in art from Sir Joshua Reynolds's *Age of Innocence* (1788) onwards. It was a theme exploited particularly by the Reverend William Peters at the close of the eighteenth century in his sentimental, slightly erotic paintings of children, and it can be traced right through the nineteenth century to the photographs by, for instance, Lewis Carroll. Innocence came to be typified above all in the repose of sleep. Hill's endless photographs of sleeping children (however useful the device may have been technically) may be compared with William Etty's *Guardian Cherubs* (figure 60), exhibited at the Royal Academy in 1828, or Henry Weekes's *Sleeping Child and Dog* (figure 61), shown at the 1851 Great Exhibition, four years after the last of the calotypes was taken.

The photographs of fisherfolk at Newhaven belong to the genre pictures. Most of them bear titles other than factual descriptions and all are conceived according to the notion that the working classes are picturesque. The pictures are not at any point animated by a social conscience but are solely arranged as compositions, mainly to show off the charming costume of the fisherwomen, who constituted a well-known feature of Edinburgh life until the end of the century (see, for example, figure 62). This is how they are described in *Chamber's Edinburgh Journal** in the 1830's:

62. Newhaven fisherwomen ("Sisters")— page 185.

> A cap of cotton or linen, surmounted by a stout napkin tied below the chin, comprises the investiture of the head. . . . A sort of woollen pea-jacket, of vast amplitude of skirt, conceals the upper part of the person, relieved at the throat by a liberal dis-

*Quoted in John Kay, *A Series of Original Portraits and Character Etchings,* volume 2 (Hugh Paton, Edinburgh, 1842).

play of handkerchief. The underpart of the figure is invested with a voluminous quantity of petticoat and gaudy colour, generally yellow with stripes, and worn in such immense numbers, that the mere mention of them would be enough to make a fine lady faint. One half of these ample garments is fastened up over the haunches, puffing out the figure in an unusual and uncouth manner. White worsted stockings and stout shoes complete the picture.

In spite of the picturesque intent, Hill incidentally manages to give us some of the earliest records we have of working-class attire in the nineteenth century.

•

Little comment can be made on the topographical views other than that the reality of a place could not be "arranged"—to use Hill's own word—in quite the same way as it could be in his own topographical paintings and lithographs, in which he always romanticized the scene and achieved his effects of distance by dramatic tree or cliff silhouettes in the foreground (figure 63). Within the albums these views represent a fair amount of travelling—from Leith to Linlithgow, Edinburgh to York and St. Andrews. Again, they are motivated in the main by a delight in the picturesque—Durham and

63. *David Octavius Hill:* Castle Campbell, *Lithograph (Courtauld Institute of Art)*.

St. Andrews cathedrals, Linlithgow Palace, the Scott Monument, and, most obsessive of all, photographs of tombs.

Twelve of the topographical views, in fact, depict tombs at Greyfriars Churchyard, Edinburgh. They are nearly all of great beauty, and one (page 68) was chosen as the frontispiece to more than one set of bound presentation albums of prints (as in the National Portrait Gallery albums). This depicts Hill seated sketching on the left, with two young women on the right, usually thought to be his nieces the Misses Morris. The choice of this calotype to open the albums as a monument to posterity (it follows his own self-portrait—see page 223) may not be without deliberate significance. The theme of *memento mori* is overt, the figures grouped around a tomb, often in the other photographs actually examining the inscription upon it. In these, Hill draws directly upon a theme which found its quintessential image in Nicolas Poussin's famous picture *Et in Arcadia ego (Even in Arcadia, I, Death, Hold Sway)*, in which Arcadian shepherds, encountering a tomb in their idyllic countryside, muse on the idea of mortality (figure 64). The tradition was alive in England in the eighteenth century when in 1769 Reynolds painted Mrs. Crewe and Mrs. Bouverie seated before a tombstone, sentimentalizing over its inscription (figure 65). Later Giovanni Battista Cipriani executed an engraving on the same subject, *Death Even in Arcady*, in which Arcadian figures gesture with alarm at the revelation of the inscription on the tomb they have discovered amidst the greenwood. To this, Hill, in his compositions in the graveyard at Greyfriars, adds the tradition of the attendant mourners, typical of funerary monuments in the eighteenth and nineteenth centuries. Without doubt the albums are meant to open with this moralistic message of the transitory nature of human life, here for a fleeting moment, gone forever at the next, and now its ephemerality made even more poignant by man's ability to make true images of himself.

•

The albums contain some of the earliest photographs to give us an entirely realistic representation of the dress of a particular period. For the periods before the advent of photography, our knowledge of clothes is restricted to the haphazard survival of actual garments and their record in pictorial sources—above all, in portraits and fashion plates. The latter are not altogether irrelevant to the study of Hill and Adamson's work. Theirs is a contrived elegance of presenta-

64. *Nicolas Poussin:* Et in Arcadia ego *(Louvre).*

65. *Sir Joshua Reynolds:* Mrs. Crewe and Mrs. Bouverie, *1769 (The Lord O'Neill).*

tion, an attention to decor and properties, which attempts to elevate the sitters into an ideal world. The visions of female beauty inspired by the school of artists responsible for the *Book of Beauty* are related to the world of fashion. Mrs. Murray trails her silken dress (page 127), and Miss Matilda Rigby deploys her parasol (figure 66) with all the art of the mannequin. How accurate, therefore, are these photographs as a record of clothes worn every day during the 1840's? The photographs, it is true, provide us with an interesting glimpse of clothes on the human figure, but as a source they are limited, because apart from the Newhaven fisherfolk the record is strictly upper class. The dress, too, is mostly summer dress, for the elementary reason that sittings took place in the open, and the busiest period for sittings was therefore of necessity during the warm summer months. One will look in vain for evidence of the capes, mantles, coats, furs, and muffs of the cold outdoors and the winter.

66. *Miss Matilda Rigby—page 117.*

Fashion for women in the 1840's was a remarkably static phenomenon. After the explosion of detail during the 1830's, the silhouette suddenly clarified and sharpened into that of an inverted triangle surmounting the dome of the skirt. The pointed waistline, established by the mid-1830's, was the norm on all dresses of the 1840's. Sleeves tightened and were so low off the shoulders that the wearers found difficulty moving. As the decade progressed the dome of the skirt expanded. This was made possible by the invention of a new method of pleating the skirt into the bodice, in which the edge of the fold alone was attached, and by the introduction of the horsehair petticoat over which several other layers of petticoats were worn. This expansion was to reach its peak in the 1850's with the introduction of the crinoline frame. Above the skirt the bodice, boned into a fan shape and back-fastened, remained static in form apart from a gradual lengthening which matched the growth in size of the skirt. The most characteristic fabric for 1840's dresses was "changeable," or shot, silk, in delicate and subtle shades, plain or figured. Dress trimmings remained remarkably restrained throughout the decade. Accessories included the parasol; gloves or mittens, which were *de rigueur*; the bonnet, made of watered silk, crêpe, straw, or rice straw for the summer and velvet for the winter; scarves of silk crêpe, gauze, black lace, and net; and shawls of cashmere, printed satin, plaid or shot silk, damasked crêpe, muslin, gauze, net, and lace.

If we turn to the Hill and Adamson photographs of female sitters, what is it that most strikes us as different from the informa-

67. Mrs. Anne Rigby—page 110;
see also pages 108, 109, 114, 115, 116.

68. Mrs. Barker—page 267.

69. Miss Kemp—page 266;
see also pages 267, 268.

tion disseminated by the modish fashion plate? Undoubtedly the most arresting feature is the actual line of the skirt. In the albums one is aware of the body beneath and in no instance does the skirt line bell out in quite the way it was optimistically depicted by the artists of the fashion plate. Rather, it falls gently, sloping from the pleats beneath the bodice, and, when a lady sits, one is definitely aware of the knees and legs beneath. Nor could any human have the bottleneck shoulder line an artist could so easily draw, ignoring the realities of female anatomy. There are also the older ladies, who, even if they are wearing the clothes of the 1840's, seem essentially to belong to the 1830's. Mrs. Anne Rigby (figure 67) is an instance of this, wearing a lace pelerine from an earlier period.

The albums also record the two main types of female hair-dressing during the 1840's. In one, the hair is parted in the middle of the brow and looped up around the ears, the hair at the back being plaited into a coiled bun (figure 68, for example). In the other, the hair is similarly parted in the middle, this time over the crown of the head also, and ironed into ringlets which cascade on either side of the face. The hair at the back sometimes was plaited into a small bun (figure 69). Both styles were singularly unflattering.

Within the National Portrait Gallery albums there is a much fuller coverage of men's than of women's dress. The full-skirted frock coat, single- or double-breasted, fastened over the front of the body and falling just below or above the knee, was the almost universal garment of every rank of society. In the few full-length portraits in the albums (figure 70, for example), this typical garment of the nineteenth century can be seen topping the narrow clinging trousers of the 1840's. The photographs give us a glimpse into the only area of men's dress to retain the riot of colour and decoration prevalent in the eighteenth century, the waistcoat, which was of coloured silk in floral or formalized patterns. Most of the waistcoats are plain, but there are occasional examples of figured, striped, and checked silk (figure 71). Throughout the 1840's, collars of shirts were gradually lowered and cravats were of black and coloured silks, both striped and figured. The albums also illustrate the decline of the cravat (patterned cravats are worn by John Murray, figure 71; Dr. James Inglis, page 210; and Dr. Samuel Smith, page 352) and the arrival of the bow tie. No sitter wears the ubiquitous cylindrical top hat (except in "Edinburgh Castle," page 248), but a number are carried (pages 147, 204). Throughout there is a representative selection

70. Lord Ruthven—page 204;
see also pages 124, 141, 143.

71. John Murray—page 126;
see also pages 206, 213, 216.

72. Master John Hope Finlay—page 284.

*73. The Misses Grierson—page 278;
see also pages 283, 285.*

of men's hair styles and side whiskers, the only marked eccentric being the sculptor John Henning (pages 129, 130, 142), who wore his white locks long and trailing over his coat collar at the back.

There is some record also of children's dress. Three pictures show a typical form of boy's dress (figure 72 and pages 279 and 283), the tunic worn over trousers. The tunic was long and belted and often made of velvet, but the albums record them in checkered woollen fabrics popular in the 1840's. One boy, Master Miller (pages 100, 275, 276), wears Highland dress of a type later to be adapted and taken up as standard boy's dress. Its popularization was due to the royal children, who wore a form of Highland dress while they were at Balmoral. Girls in the albums follow in miniature the silhouettes of their mothers, except that the skirts are shorter. By the 1840's the bodice of a girl's dress was generally longer than its skirt. Low-cut dresses with short sleeves are recorded as fashionable wear for little girls, but the photographs show that Edinburgh mothers sensibly kept their daughters buttoned up to the neck (for example, figure 73). Hair styles followed those of their elders, being either parted in the middle and looped back over the ears or falling to the shoulders in ringlets. None of the girls wears a bonnet; they wear instead hats with wide brims and flat crowns, which were particularly favoured for the country.

This, then, is what Hill and Adamson's photographs tell us of fashions in the 1840's. In a way, it is a limited picture, for, in the case of his women sitters, Hill may be said to be the first fashion photographer, with all the artificiality which that implies. If we study his photographs, we find that not only was he inspired by the keepsake votive images of the 1840's in his vision of early Victorian womanhood, he was also directly trying, in some specific instances, to photograph dress alone. Portraits such as the back views of Mrs. Murray (page 127) and Lady Ruthven (figure 74) are records of clothes and not primarily of personalities; Hill is in fact arranging his ladies in the poses recurring in the innumerable fashion plates that originated in Paris and circulated throughout Europe. Although the back views may evoke for us the silken dresses of ladies in the paintings of Pieter de Hooch and Gerard Terborch, a source closer to nineteenth-century reality is a typical print such as that showing morning visiting and walking dresses for *The Ladies' Cabinet* of 1844 (figure 75). Similarly, the modish picture of Miss Elizabeth Rigby with her mother (page 116) has an exact parallel in fashion

74. Lady Ruthven—page 205.

*75. Morning Visiting and Walking Dresses
(The Ladies' Cabinet, 1844).*

76. Demi-Toilette and Public Promenade Dress (The Ladies' Cabinet, *1844*).

prints such as that depicting demi-toilette and public promenade dress in the same publication for the same year (figure 76).

•

What is it finally which makes the contents of the National Portrait Gallery albums so hypnotic as images? Analysis seems to reduce them almost to the level of crude derivations of academic formulae of the day. But Adamson's calotypes without Hill are dull and Hill's without Adamson even duller. Some extraordinary chemistry must have been at work between these two men during the four and a half years of their association. The very novelty of the technique was on their side, but if one has to explain the inherent strength of their vision, one comes to the conclusion that it is because through Hill's "arrangement" they produced images belonging to the tradition of the Grand Manner. The best of their work seems to gather to itself the achievements of Scottish painting in the golden age of Raeburn and Wilkie and, by dint of the novel medium, to give it a final and most glorious lustre.

THE FIRST GENERAL ASSEMBLY

OF THE FREE CHURCH OF SCOTLAND

Signing the Act of Separation and Deed of Demission,

at Tanfield, Edinburgh, May, 1843

———————

A Painting by D. O. Hill, R.S.A.

*[Greyfriars Churchyard, with D. O. Hill—
from the title page of Volume I of the National Portrait Gallery albums]*

I, 2   211 × 160 mm   8$\frac{5}{16}$ × 6$\frac{5}{16}$ inches

THE ALBUMS

A NOTE ABOUT THE CAPTIONS

Hill's own wording is used wherever it exists and is legible. Supplementary information, including birth and death dates, has been added in brackets.

The volume and number of each original in the National Portrait Gallery albums, and its approximate size in millimeters and inches, are to be found below each caption. In general, plates are arranged within each section in the order in which they appear in the National Portrait Gallery albums—for example, calotype I, 8 follows calotype I, 6; and II, 2 follows I, 99. This arrangement, however, is sometimes altered—as on pages 289–303, where various portraits of the same person have been grouped together for the reader's convenience.

As all the calotypes were taken within a period of four and one half years, there is little development in technique between the first and the last, though some improvement in clarity and definition is discernible. Precise dating is therefore of little more than academic interest. Nevertheless, where such information is known, it also has been included in brackets.

To the
President and Members
of the
Royal Academy of Fine Arts;
London.

These attempts to apply artistically,
the recently discovered process of

The Calotype,

Are, with great respect,
Inscribed and presented
by their
Obedient Humble Servant,

D. O. Hill.

Edinburgh,
26ᵗʰ July, 1846.

THE
DISRUPTION
PAINTING

Hill's mammoth painting *The First General Assembly of the Free Church of Scotland, Signing the Act of Separation and Deed of Demission, at Tanfield, Edinburgh, May, 1843* is reproduced on pages 66–7. Less than half the faces in it can be identified in Hill and Adamson's preparatory calotypes, but thirty of these pictures—in the National Portrait Gallery albums and reproduced in this section—are of individuals posed exactly as in the painting. Different poses will be found in appropriate sections elsewhere. Adamson's face in the painting is derived from a calotype group of the Adamson family (page 229) and it seemed more apt to include this in the section devoted to Hill, Adamson, and their families.

Among the many painted likenesses of people not present at the Disruption are all those in the left-hand skylight: the sculptors John Henning and Alexander Handyside Ritchie (page 78), a Newhaven fisherman, Willie Liston (page 103), and a fishwife, perhaps Mrs. Barbara Flucker (page 169). The face of Master James Miller (page 100) is reversed in the painting.

The photograph of Thomas Chalmers (page 74) is the only one in all three albums that has a border.

The Revd Thomas Chalmers [1780–1847] *D. D.*
[*the first Moderator of the Free Church*]

I, 6   170 × 127 mm   6¹¹⁄₁₆ × 5 inches

Robert Cunningham Graham Spiers Esq. [1797–1847],
Sheriff of Edinburghshire [Midlothian]

I, 8   195 × 142 mm   7¹¹⁄₁₆ × 5⁹⁄₁₆ inches

Dr [Alexander] Keith [1791–1880],
Author of Several Works on the Prophetic Writings

I, 12   199 × 131 mm   7⅞ × 5³⁄₁₆ inches

[The] Revd Dr [David] Welsh [1793–1845,
outgoing Moderator of the Church of Scotland,
who read out the Act of Protest]

I, 14   146 × 115 mm   5¾ × 4⁹⁄₁₆ inches

John Henning [1771–1851]
and A. H. [Alexander Handyside] Ritchie [1804–70]
Sculptors

I, 24   201 × 149 mm 7¹⁵⁄₁₆ × 5⅞ inches

Dr [Abraham] Capadose
[1795–1874, physician and Calvinist writer, of The Hague]

I, 26   201 × 149 mm   7¹⁵⁄₁₆ × 5⅞ inches

[The] Revd [D.] T. K. Drummond
[1799–1888, B.A., Episcopalian minister from London]

I, 39   198 × 153 mm   7¹³⁄₁₆ × 6¹⁄₁₆ inches

[The] Revd J. Julius Wood [1800–77,
of Greyfriars Church, Edinburgh, and Malta, photographed October 22nd, 1843]

I, 45   204 × 147 mm   8 × 5$\frac{13}{16}$ inches

[The] Revd Dr [Jabez] Bunting
[1779–1851, a prominent Wesleyan Methodist from London]

I, 47   202 × 153 mm $7^{15}/_{16}$ × $6^{1}/_{16}$ inches

Professor [Alexander Campbell] Fraser [1819–1914],
New College, Edinburgh

I, 51   193 × 142 mm   7⅝ × 5⁹⁄₁₆ inches

[The] Revd Dr [James] Brewster [1777–1847],
Craig, Fife [Sir David Brewster's elder brother]

I, 54   202 × 147 mm   7¹⁵⁄₁₆ × 5¹³⁄₁₆ inches

Mr John Duncan, Perth
[music master, brother of Thomas Duncan]

I, 56   193 × 142 mm   7⅝ × 5 9/16 inches

[The] Revd Fred^k [Frédéric Joël Jean Gerard] Monod [1794–1863],
Paris [founder of the Free French Reformed Church]

I, 61   201 × 143 mm   7$^{15}/_{16}$ × 5$^5/_8$ inches

[The] Revd [William] Govan

[1804–75, Glasgow Missionary Society, missionary in the Cape (South Africa)]

I, 62   196 × 137 mm   7¹¹⁄₁₆ × 5⁷⁄₁₆ inches

[The] Revd Thos [Thomas Blizzard] Bell [1815–66],
Free Church, Leswalt [brother of Dr George Bell]

I, 64   196 × 147 mm $7\frac{11}{16}$ × $5\frac{13}{16}$ inches

88

Uncle Tom (Mr Thomas Miller, Edinburgh) [*D. O. Hill's uncle*]

I, 66   151 × 122 mm $5^{15}/_{16}$ × $4^{13}/_{16}$ inches

[Alexander] Thomson [1798–1868], Esq. of Banchory

I, 68   200 × 152 mm   7⅞ × 6 inches

Dr George [William] Bell
[medical doctor and social reformer,
brother of the Reverend Thomas Bell]

I, 70   194 × 142 mm   7⅝ × 5⁹⁄₁₆ inches

[The] Revd Mr [Joseph] Thorburn [1799–1854],
Free Church, Inverness

1, 76   204 × 146 mm   8 × 5¾ inches

Mr [David] Maitland McGill Crichton
[1801–44(?), Fife landowner, a lay leader of the Free Church]

I, 81   200 × 145 mm   7⅞ × 5¾ inches

Thomas Duncan [1807–45],
R. S. A., A. R. A. [portraitist and history painter]

I, 84   143 × 108 mm   5⅝ × 4¼ inches

[The] Revd Andrew Gray
[1805–61, minister of West Church], Perth

I, 85   198 × 142 mm   7¹³⁄₁₆ × 5⁹⁄₁₆ inches

Dr [William Hamilton] Burns [1779–1859], Kilsyth
[his son, Professor Islay Burns, is also shown in the Disruption painting]

I, 86   194 × 141 mm   7⅝ × 5⁹⁄₁₆ inches

[The] Revd Mr [George] Lewis [1803–79], Dundee

I, 99   210 × 155 mm   8¼ × 6⅛ inches

Free Church Committee; the Marquis of Bre[a]dalbane,
Sir David Brewster, Dr [David] Welsh, [Mr John] Hamilton of Ninewar
and Sheriff [A. Earle] Monteith

II, 2   144 × 199 mm   5¹¹⁄₁₆ × 7⅞ inches

Study for part of a picture of
the first General Assembly of the Free Church
[with the Reverend Dr George Muirhead, 1764–1847;
Dr William Cunningham, 1805–61;
the Reverend Dr James Begg, 1808–83;
Dr Thomas Guthrie, 1803–73;
Mr John Hamilton, 1799–1851]

II, 3   89 × 105 mm   3½ × 4⅛ inches

Master [James] Miller [1837–68, eldest son of Professor James Miller]

II, 35   194 × 139 mm   7⅝ × 5½ inches

Dundee Free Church Presbytery
[*with the Miller family, Glasgow, photographed October 18th, 1843*]

II, 38   144 × 196 mm $5^{11}/_{16}$ × $7^{11}/_{16}$ inches

[The] Revd Mr Moir [see page 32]
and John Gibson [1799–1871, Her Majesty's Inspector of Schools]

II, 52   197 × 143 mm   7¾ × 5⅝ inches

Baiting the Line
[*Willie Liston, Newhaven, probably photographed in June 1845*]

III, 37   186 × 137 mm   7⁵⁄₁₆ × 5⁷⁄₁₆ inches

———

MRS. RIGBY

AND HER DAUGHTERS

Anne Palgrave, daughter of William Palgrave of Yarmouth, married Dr. Edward Rigby of Norwich and bore him twelve children. He died in 1822, but she survived him by fifty years. Amongst the twelve children were Elizabeth and Matilda, who appear on the following pages. In October 1842 Mrs. Rigby and these two daughters went to live in Edinburgh.

Elizabeth wrote on the arts and worked for a time for John Murray, the publisher (page 126), at whose house she met Hill. She was impressed by Hill and Adamson's calotypes and went often to Rock House—with and without her mother and sister Matilda. In 1849 Elizabeth married Charles Eastlake (later Sir Charles), President of the Royal Academy of Arts, Director of the National Gallery, and first President of the Royal Photographic Society. Although she thus became an influential figure in the London art world, she nevertheless continued to visit Edinburgh frequently. The pictures of her with a crucifix and other properties portray perhaps some character or scene of the literary type that Hill liked so much. The calotypes show that these three Rigby ladies possessed considerable strength of character and personality.

Miss Elizabeth Rigby [*1809–93, later Lady Eastlake*]

II, 22   208 × 156 mm   8³⁄₁₆ × 6⅛ inches

Miss E. [Elizabeth] Rigby

II, 23   207 × 155 mm   8³⁄₁₆ × 6⅛ inches

_____

107

Mrs Rigby [*née Anne Palgrave, 1777–1872, Elizabeth and Matilda's mother*]

II, 24   203 × 155 mm   8 × 6⅛ inches

Mrs Rigby

II, 25   207 × 159 mm   8³⁄₁₆ × 6¼ inches

109

[Mrs Rigby wearing a lace pelerine]

II, 26   212 × 158 mm   8⁵⁄₁₆ × 6³⁄₁₆ inches

Miss Matilda Rigby [later Mrs Smith, younger sister of Elizabeth]

II, 27   212 × 156 mm   8⁵⁄₁₆ × 6⅛ inches

Miss E. [Elizabeth] Rigby [photographed in 1844 or 1845]

II, 28   205 × 151 mm   8⅟₁₆ × 5¹⁵⁄₁₆ inches

Miss Matilda Rigby

II, 29   209 × 148 mm   8¼ × 5¹³⁄₁₆ inches

[Mrs Rigby—untitled by Hill]

II, 30   205 × 152 mm   8¹⁄₁₆ × 6 inches

[Mrs Rigby, photographed in 1844 or 1845]

II, 31   207 × 154 mm   8³⁄₁₆ × 6¹⁄₁₆ inches

115

Mrs Rigby and Miss E. [Elizabeth] Rigby

II, 32   201 × 148 mm   7¹⁵⁄₁₆ × 5¹³⁄₁₆ inches

—————

116

Miss Matilda Rigby

II, 33   204 × 152 mm   8 × 6 inches

Miss E. [Elizabeth] Rigby

II, 34   192 × 144 mm   7⁹⁄₁₆ × 5¹¹⁄₁₆ inches

───

118

Miss E. [Elizabeth] Rigby

II, 61   190 × 139 mm   7½ × 5½ inches

119

ARTISTS
AND FRIENDS

Most of Hill's friends were artists—many, like him, had trained at the Trustees' Academy School of Design and belonged to the Royal Scottish Academy, of which he was secretary. Two of the most photographed of Hill's artist friends were men of humble origin, Scotsmen who were largely self-taught.

John Henning, over seventy years old at the time of the calotypes, had taught himself to make wax medallions of the people of Paisley, his home town, fifty years earlier and took this up professionally about 1800. Later he studied at the School of Design and in 1811 he went to London, where his subjects included Sarah Siddons and Princess Charlotte. He made reduced copies (some in bas-relief) of the Elgin Marbles (see page 146), and his relief friezes on the same theme can still be seen on two London buildings by Decimus Burton: the Athenaeum Club and the Screen at Hyde Park Corner (his two sons also worked on this). Some of Henning's medallions and preparatory chalk drawings are in the National Portrait Gallery.

James Ballantine was a house painter who took part-time lessons at the School of Design. He revived the art of glass painting and designed the windows for Sir Charles Barry's new House of Lords. He also wrote poems and stories, including "The Gaberlunzie Man," a story for children (referred to in Hill's caption on page 149). A gaberlunzie man was a wandering mendicant or jack-of-all-trades; Sir Walter Scott used the term to describe Edie Ochiltree in his novel *The Antiquary*—see the section "Dressing Up," page 287.

John Harden (page 138), who remained an amateur artist all his life, has left a rare written description of being photographed by Hill and Adamson. In a letter dated November 14th, 1843, he tells his daughter Jessie that "I sat 3 various attitudes & 3 portraits taken price £1. 1. as not yet to be shown. I hope they may please some of my Children."

William Etty [1787–1849], R.A.
[prolific painter, especially of nudes; photographed in October 1844]

I, 7   199 × 149 mm   7⅞ × 5⅞ inches

Sir William Allan [1782–1850], *R.A.*
[second] *President of the Royal Scottish Academy of Fine Arts*

I, 9 202 × 148 mm 7^{15}/$_{16}$ × 5^{13}/$_{16}$ inches

Thomas Duncan [1807–45], R.S.A., A.R.A.
[portraitist, theatre and history painter]

I, 20   194 × 139 mm   7⅝ × 5½ inches

Sir Francis Grant [1803–78], *A.R.A.*

[*President of the Royal Academy, photographed in September 1845*]

I, 25   201 × 144 mm   7¹⁵⁄₁₆ × 5¹¹⁄₁₆ inches

Mr John Murray [*III, 1808–92*], *Albemarle Street*
[*London publisher of David Livingstone, Charles Darwin, and many others*]

I, 27   202 × 147 mm   7$^{15}/_{16}$ × 5$^{13}/_{16}$ inches

<hr />

Mrs [Marian] Murray [d. 1894, married John Murray, the publisher, in 1847]

II, 6   201 × 164 mm   7$\frac{15}{16}$ × 6$\frac{7}{16}$ inches

27

Miss Murray [*one of John Murray III's four sisters*]

II, 13   194 × 143 mm   7⅝ × 5⅝ inches

John Henning [1771–1851]

I, 31   203 × 153 mm   8 × 6¹⁄₁₆ inches

John Henning, Sculptor

I, 32   207 × 155 mm   8³⁄₁₆ × 6⅛ inches

A. H. [Alexander Handyside] Ritchie [1804–70, A.R.S.A.], Sculptor

I, 33   179 × 145 mm   7 1/16 × 5 3/4 inches

James Drummond [1816–77], A.R.S.A.
[painter, Curator of the Scottish National Gallery from 1868]

I, 34   199 × 142 mm   7⅞ × 5⁹⁄₁₆ inches

Sir William Allan, R.A., P.R.S.A.

I, 35   198 × 140 mm   7¹³⁄₁₆ × 5½ inches

133

[Sir] John Steell [1804–91], Sculptor
[among his works, the statues of Sir Walter Scott in the Scott Monument
and of Robert Burns in Westminster Abbey]

I, 52   189 × 136 mm   7⁷⁄₁₆ × 5⅜ inches

Sir W. [William] Allan, R.A., P.R.S.A. [photographed in 1844]

I, 55   197 × 140 mm   7¾ × 5½ inches

John Stevens [1793–1868], *R.S.A.* [with his sculpture The Last of the Romans]

I, 57   202 × 154 mm   7¹⁵⁄₁₆ × 6¹⁄₁₆ inches

Mr John Duncan, Perth

I, 69   193 × 146 mm   7⅝ × 5¾ inches

Mr [John] Harden [1772–1847(?),
amateur Lake District painter, photographed November 1843]

I, 71   205 × 143 mm   8$\frac{1}{16}$ × 5$\frac{5}{8}$ inches

138

Thomas Duncan, R.S.A., A.R.A.

I, 72   181 × 136 mm   7⅛ × 5⅜ inches

Jas [James] Ballantine [1808–77], Author of the Gaberlunzie's Wallet
[and stained glass artist—for example, in the House of Lords]

I, 82   210 × 156 mm   8¼ × 6⅛ inches

David Roberts [1796–1864], R.A. [popular genre painter,
photographed between the Dennistoun and Nasmyth tombs, Greyfriars, Edinburgh, September 1844]

I, 90   211 × 155 mm   8⁵⁄₁₆ × 6⅛ inches

John Henning, Sculptor

I, 92   198 × 144 mm   7¹³⁄₁₆ × 5¹¹⁄₁₆ inches

John Stevens, R.S.A.

[note, at left, his cylindrical top hat, a frequent prop in the calotypes]

I, 93   193 × 139 mm   7⅝ × 5½ inches

James Ballantine, Author

I, 95   207 × 156 mm   8³⁄₁₆ × 6⅛ inches

*Dr Geo [George William] Bell, Miss E. Bell [later Lady Moncrieff]
and [the] Revd Thos [Thomas Blizzard] Bell [1815–66, of Leswalt]*

I, 97   196 × 144 mm $7^{11}/_{16}$ × $5^{11}/_{16}$ inches

The Torso: [John] Henning, [Alexander Handyside] Ritchie and D. O. Hill
[with a reduced-size copy made by Henning from the Elgin Marbles]

I, 98   195 × 147 mm   7¹¹⁄₁₆ × 5¹³⁄₁₆ inches

146

D. O. Hill, R.S.A., W. Borthwick Johnstone [1804–68], *R.S.A.*

[*librarian, 1853–57, and treasurer, 1856–68, of the Royal Scottish Academy*]

I, 100   192 × 142 mm   7⁹⁄₁₆ × 5⁹⁄₁₆ inches

_____

Kenneth Macleay [1802–78], R.S.A.

[miniaturist and founder-member of the Royal Scottish Academy]

I, 101   154 × 109 mm   6$\frac{1}{16}$ × 4$\frac{5}{16}$ inches

'Edinburgh Ale': Jas [James] Ballantine (the Gaberlunzie), Dr Geo [George William] Bell & D. O. Hill

II, 39   144 × 199 mm   5¹¹⁄₁₆ × 7⅞ inches

Jas [James] and Thos [Thomas] Duncan, R.S.A.

II, 40   110 × 139   4⅚⁄₁₆ × 5½ inches

_____

150

A Discussion: Jas [James] Ballantine—D. O. Hill—Dr Geo [George William] Bell

II, 41   134 × 200 mm   5¼ × 7⅞ inches

The Morning after 'He Greatly Daring Dined'
[*D. O. Hill and Professor James Miller, 1812–64*]

II, 53   200 × 151 mm   7⅞ × 5¹⁵⁄₁₆ inches

The Dance—from a Picture by [William] Etty

II, 78   134 × 192 mm   5¼ × 7%6 inches

NEWHAVEN

Dr. James Fairbairn, who took part in the Disruption of the Church of Scotland and may have met Hill when the latter was first taking photographs for the Disruption painting, was ordained minister of the newly established Newhaven church in January 1838. Most of his congregation were fishermen and women and he took a special interest in their welfare.

Having soon raised the money to build a church (previously the congregation had shared one about a mile and a half away), Fairbairn tackled the problem of getting their boats fitted with proper decks and cabins; it is possible that Hill and Adamson's calotypes of Newhaven were taken in connection with this highly successful campaign.

Fairbairn himself appears in "The Pastor's Visit" (page 179), which seems to have been taken outside Rock House rather than in Newhaven itself. Behind him stands James Gall, Sr., an Edinburgh publisher who pioneered the use of braille in Scotland, and the women include (left to right) Mrs. Carnie Noble, Bessie Crombie, Mary Comble, and Mrs. Lyle.

Hill sometimes captions "King Fisher" (page 164) "His feyther's breeks he hath girded on," and Mrs. Elizabeth Johnstone (pages 166, 168, 176) "A Newhaven Beauty."

The Beach at Newhaven [near Edinburgh]

III, 3   133 × 189 mm   5¼ × 7⁷⁄₁₆ inches

Fisher Laddies [*probably photographed in June 1845*]

III, 4   135 × 186 mm   5⅝₁₆ × 7⅝₁₆ inches

Fishermen at Home

III, 5   142 × 195 mm   5⁹⁄₁₆ × 7¹¹⁄₁₆ inches

Fishermen

III, 6 111 × 159 mm 4⅜ × 6¼ inches

Newhaven Pilot's Cottage Door

III, 7   140 × 194 mm   5½ × 7⅝ inches

160

Newhaven Fisher Callants ["*young men*"]

III, 8   137 × 191 mm   5⅞₁₆ × 7⁹₁₆ inches

[*Three Fisherwomen*]

III, 9   143 × 194 mm   5⅝ × 7⅝ inches

Fisher Lassies

III, 10   195 × 141 mm   7$\frac{11}{16}$ × 5$\frac{9}{16}$ inches

163

King Fisher, Newhaven

III, 11   197 × 144 mm   7¾ × 5¹¹⁄₁₆ inches

164

Newhaven Fisherman

III, 12   146 × 111 mm   5¾ × 4⅜ inches

165

Mrs Elizabeth Johnstone, Newhaven

III, 13   191 × 146 mm   7⁹⁄₁₆ × 5¾ inches

Newhaven Pilot

III, 14   193 × 139 mm   7⅝ × 5½ inches

[Mrs] Elizabeth Johnstone

III, 15   191 × 146 mm   7⁹⁄₁₆ × 5¾ inches

[Mrs Barbara Flucker, the oysterwoman]

III, 16   200 × 148 mm   7⅞ × 5¹³⁄₁₆ inches

[Mrs Barbara Flucker, the oysterwoman]

III, 17   201 × 148 mm   7$\frac{15}{16}$ × 5$\frac{13}{16}$ inches

[Fishermen—Hill's title illegible]

III, 18   143 × 203 mm   5⅝ × 8 inches

Sandy [James] Linton, his boat and his bairns

III, 19   196 × 142 mm   7$\frac{11}{16}$ × 5$\frac{9}{16}$ inches

Jeanie Wilson and Annie Linton

III, 20   187 × 143 mm   7⅜ × 5⅝ inches

173

Fisher Lassie and Child

III, 21   187 × 143 mm   7⅜ × 5⅝ inches

174

The Letter [*Marion Finlay, Margaret Dryburgh, and Grace Finlay*]

III, 22   191 × 138 mm   7⁹⁄₁₆ × 5⁷⁄₁₆ inches

Love Reverie [*Mrs Elizabeth Johnstone*]

III, 23   190 × 141 mm   7½ × 5⁹⁄₁₆ inches

Fisher Lassies
[*including Marion Finlay, Margaret Dryburgh, and Grace Finlay*]

III, 24   144 × 200 mm   5¹¹⁄₁₆ × 7⅞ inches

———

Fisher Lassies

III, 25   144 × 198 mm   5¹¹⁄₁₆ × 7¹³⁄₁₆ inches

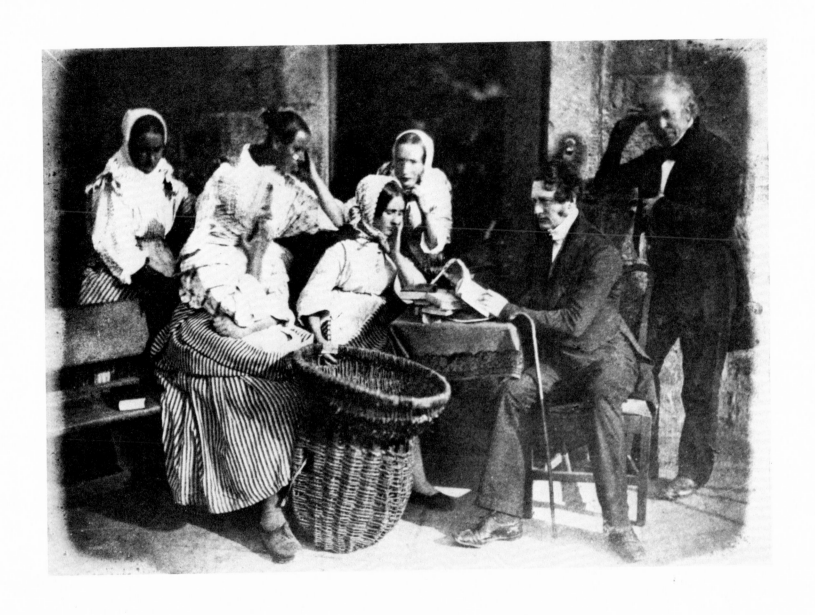

The Pastor's Visit

[*with the Reverend James Fairbairn—see page 155*]

III, 26   144 × 199 mm   5¹¹⁄₁₆ × 7⅞ inches

Jeanie Wilson

III, 27   199 × 141 mm   7⅞ × 5⁹⁄₁₆ inches

English Yachtmen and Newhaven Fishermen

III, 28   143 × 197 mm   5⅝ × 7¾ inches

181

Fisherwomen [also called "A Lane in Newhaven"]

III, 29   151 × 197 mm   5¹⁵⁄₁₆ × 7¾ inches

Two Fishermen

III, 30   143 × 107 mm   5⅝ × 4¼ inches

Fisher Lass

III, 31   152 × 109 mm   6 × 4⁵⁄₁₆ inches

Sisters

III, 32   190 × 141 mm   7½ × 5⁹⁄₁₆ inches

_____

185

[Two Fisherwomen]

III, 33   291 × 212 mm   11$\frac{7}{16}$ × 8$\frac{5}{16}$ inches

Cottage Door

III, 34   198 × 143 mm   7¹³⁄₁₆ × 5⅝ inches

Fishermen Ashore
[*Alex Rutherford, William Ramsay, and John Liston*]

III, 35   189 × 137 mm   7⁷⁄₁₆ × 5⁷⁄₁₆ inches

Home from Market

III, 36   186 × 138 mm   7⁵⁄₁₆ × 5⁷⁄₁₆ inches

Just Landed

III, 38   196 × 140 mm   7¹¹⁄₁₆ × 5½ inches

Fisher Laddies [*sometimes called "The Fry"*]

III, 39   180 × 130 mm   7 1/16 × 5 1/8 inches

WORTHY AND FAMOUS
MEN AND WOMEN

Hill came into contact with everyone in Edinburgh society, as well as its most distinguished visitors. Many of these acquaintances were photographed at Rock House. In October 1844, during the second year of their partnership, Hill and Adamson went to the York meeting of the British Association for the Advancement of Science, and among the calotypes made there are those of the Marquis of Northampton (page 195), President of the Royal Society from 1838 to 1849, and of Dr. James Inglis (page 210), author of *A Treatise on the English Bronchocele, Giving the Principal Localities of the Disease and Its Apparent Causes, with Remarks on the Use of Iodine* (1838). According to a letter written by John Harden (page 138) to his daughter Jessie on November 14th, 1843, it was he who persuaded John Wilson (page 196) to sit: "Professor Wilson comes with me at 2 on Friday & I hope to get him to give 5 minutes—a famous subject."

Less well-known outside Scotland was George Gunn (page 212), chief, from 1814 until his death in 1859, of the Gunn clan, which still thrives in Caithness and Sutherland. By coincidence, the Gunn connection with Hill and Adamson continues: all the pictures in this book were reproduced from negatives made by a present-day member of the clan.

The [second] Marquis of Northampton [Spencer Joshua Alwyne Compton, 1790–1851, Member of Parliament for Northampton, 1812–20, and President of the Royal Society, 1838–48, photographed in York, October 28th, 1844]

I, 3   198 × 137 mm   7¹³⁄₁₆ × 5⁷⁄₁₆ inches

John Wilson Esq. [1785–1854], *Professor of Moral Philosophy,*
Edinburgh University, Editor of Blackwood's Magazine
[*photographed in November 1843*]

I, 4   193 × 143 mm   7⅝ × 5⅝ inches

Sir David Brewster

[1781–1868, who introduced Hill to Adamson in 1843]

I, 10   194 × 144 mm   7⅝ × 5¹¹⁄₁₆ inches

197

Sir John McNeill [*1795–1883*], *G.C.B.*
[*surgeon and diplomat, photographed August 18th, 1845*]

I, 11   203 × 149 mm   8 × 5⅞ inches

Dr [Alexander] Monro [tertius, *1773–1859*],
Professor of Anatomy in Edinburgh University

I, 15   203 × 150 mm   8 × 5⅞ inches

Dr [Alexander] Monro, Professor of Anatomy, Edinburgh University

I, 16   207 × 153 mm   8¹³⁄₁₆ × 6¹⁄₁₆ inches

[The] Hon Francis [Wemyss-] Charteris [-Douglas, 1818–1914], M.P.
[Lord Elcho, later tenth Earl of Wemyss]

I, 17   202 × 148 mm   7¹⁵/₁₆ × 5¹³/₁₆ inches

Robert Liston Esq. [1794–1847], *Surgeon*
[*F.R.S., Professor of Clinical Surgery, University of London*]

I, 18   214 × 150 mm   8⁷⁄₁₆ × 5⁷⁄₈ inches

Robert Liston, Esq., Surgeon

I, 19   203 × 149 mm   8 × 5⅞ inches

Lord Ruthven [*1777–1853, of Winton, photographed in 1845*]

I, 22   204 × 146 mm   8 × 5¾ inches

Lady Ruthven [1789–1885, Mary, wife of Lord Ruthven and friend of Sir Walter Scott]

II, 12   204 × 152 mm   8 × 6 inches

[The] Hon Jas [James Archibald] Stuart-Wortley [1805–81], M. P.
[Queen's Counsel, Solicitor-General 1856–57 under Lord Palmerston]

I, 23   204 × 159 mm   8 × 6¼ inches

[The] Hon Mr & Mrs Jas [James] Stuart-Wortley [photographed in 1846]

I, 102   201 × 151 mm $7\frac{15}{16}$ × $5\frac{15}{16}$ inches

James Nasmyth [*1808–1890*], *Inventor of the Steam Hammer* [*in 1839, photographed about 1844*]

I, 28   194 × 152 mm   7⅝ × 6 inches

[James Aytoun of Kirkcaldy, Chartist, manufacturer,
Radical candidate for Edinburgh, 1839–40]

I, 36   205 × 141 mm   8 1/16 × 5 5/16 inches

Dr [James] Inglis [1813–51], Halifax
[specialist in treating goitre, photographed in York in 1844]

I, 37   206 × 152 mm   8⅛ × 6 inches

Dr [George] Buist [1805–60], Editor of the Bombay Times *[photographed in 1845]*

I, 41   202 × 141 mm   7¹⁵⁄₁₆ × 5⁹⁄₁₆ inches

Mr [George] Gunn [d. 1859], Factor to the Duke of Sutherland
[at Dunrobin, chief of the Gunn clan from 1814 to 1859]
[A duplicate of this calotype—numbered I, 78, measuring 196 × 144 mm—
is also included in the National Portrait Gallery albums]

I, 44   193 × 140 mm   7⅝ × 5½ inches

Col [James Glencairn] Burns [1794–1865], Youngest Son of the Poet [Robert Burns]

I, 50   200 × 151 mm   7⅞ × 5¹⁵⁄₁₆ inches

James Miller [1812–64], *Professor of Surgery, Edinburgh* [*University*]

I, 58   190 × 146 mm   7½ × 5¾ inches

Lord Robertson [1794–1855, Scottish judge and author]

I, 74   206 × 148 mm   8⅛ × 5¹³⁄₁₆ inches

[Robert Stephen] Rintoul, Esq. [1787–1858] of The Spectator
[which he founded and edited]

I, 79   198 × 149 mm   7¹³⁄₁₆ × 5⅞ inches

[Dr] George Combe

[1788–1858, Writer to the Signet, phrenologist, and author; married Sarah Siddons's daughter]

I, 87   203 × 152 mm   8 × 6 inches

Mr [Robert] Liston, Surgeon

I, 91   207 × 154 mm   8³⁄₁₆ × 6¹⁄₁₆ inches

[Mrs Anna Brownell Jameson, 1794–1860, née Murphy, writer and art critic]

II, 10   202 × 137 mm   7^{15}/$_{16}$ × 5^{7}/$_{16}$ inches

HILL AND ADAMSON
AND THEIR FAMILIES

David Hill appears in at least a dozen of the calotypes, but this section includes only the portraits.

Throughout his four-and-a-half-year partnership with Robert Adamson, Hill was a widower, so there is no photograph of either of his wives, but there is one of his daughter, Charlotte (page 226). Another picture, "A Study" (page 269), is often identified as being of her but, since the sitter is obviously much older than Charlotte (whose ninth birthday was a few days after Adamson's death), this is not possible. Hill's sister Mary Watson (page 225), with whom he went to live after his first wife died, was the widow of Professor Dr. Watson, of Brechan, Fife, a surgeon who had served at Trafalgar, and a close friend of Sir William Hamilton, Professor of Moral Philosophy at Edinburgh University.

The only pictures of Adamson in the National Portrait Gallery albums are included here; that of his family (page 229) shows (*standing*) Alexander, Mrs. John Adamson, and Dr. John Adamson; (*sitting*) Mrs. Bell (wife of Colonel Bell) of Madras, Melville Adamson (subject of John's first calotype portrait), and Robert.

[D. O. Hill, 1802–70, photographed about 1843]

I, 1   197 × 137 mm   7¾ × 5⁷⁄₁₆ inches

[David Octavius Hill]

II, 1   208 × 153 mm   8¾₁₆ × 6⅛₁₆ inches

My sister, Mrs Mary Watson

II, 4   194 × 152 mm   7⅝ × 6 inches

Charlotte [1839–62]—only child of D. O. Hill

II, 73   148 × 200 mm   5¹³⁄₁₆ × 7⅞ inches

Mrs Charles Finlay [a niece of Hill's]

II, 16   194 × 144 mm   7⅝ × 5¹¹⁄₁₆ inches

227

Miss Patricia Morris [later Mrs Orr, Mrs Finlay's sister; d. 1854]

II, 11   210 × 153 mm   8¼ × 6⅟₁₆ inches

The Adamson family [photographed in 1844 or 1845—see page 221]

II, 51   183 × 143 mm   7³⁄₁₆ × 5⁵⁄₈ inches

Robert Adamson, Calotypist, Born 1821, Died 1848

III, 1   201 × 144 mm   7$^{15}/_{16}$ × 5$^{11}/_{16}$ inches

Mrs Bell, Madras [*one of Adamson's sisters*]

II, 17   202 × 152 mm   7¹⁵⁄₁₆ × 6 inches

EDINBURGH

Over half the calotypes in this section were taken in Greyfriars Churchyard, in Edinburgh, whose mainly seventeenth-century tombs appealed to Hill's love of the romantic and picturesque. Human beings were used as set dressings in all these photographs, and Hill seems to figure in most of them.

The pictures of the Scott Monument constitute a record of its building from foundation (page 248), through erection (page 251— one of the largest calotypes in the National Portrait Gallery albums), to completion (pages 247, 252–3). It is fairly certain that one of the two top-hatted men in "Edinburgh Castle" (page 248) is George Meikle Kemp, its architect, who died in 1844, two years before it was finished. Kemp's sister was also photographed by Hill and Adamson (page 266). "John Knox's House" (page 245) may have been taken at the instigation of Lord Cockburn, a campaigner for the conservation of old Edinburgh, as was Hill's friend Dr. George Bell, who published pamphlets on *Day and Night in the Wynds of Edinburgh* and *Blackfriars Wynd Analyzed* (the wynds are the narrow streets of the old town). "Leith Docks" (page 250) shows two of the artillerymen stationed there, in full dress uniform.

[Sir Robert] Dennistoun's Tomb, Greyfriars [Churchyard] Edinburgh
[Hill, with sketchpad, at left]

III, 40   205 × 144 mm   8⅜ × 5¹¹⁄₁₆ inches

The Covenanters' Tomb, Greyfriars
[with *Hill and one of the Misses Watson (?)*]

III, 41   194 × 133 mm   7⅝ × 5¼ inches

A Tomb in the Greyfriars, Edinburgh

III, 42   193 × 132 mm   7⁹⁄₁₆ × 5³⁄₁₆ inches

The Greyfriars, Edinburgh
[*the west wall, with Hill (?) and Thomas Duncan (?)*]

III, 43   113 × 157 mm   4⁷⁄₁₆ × 6³⁄₁₆ inches

The Mylnes' Tomb—'Here are buried four of the Master Architects
or Master Builders to the Successive Scottish Monarchs'

III, 44   205 × 153 mm   8¹⁄₁₆ × 6¹⁄₁₆ inches

Tombs in the Greyfriars [Churchyard; as always, human figures are included]

III, 45   155 × 210 mm   6⅛ × 8¼ inches

The Greyfriars, Edinburgh
[*with three men, one of whom is possibly Hill*]

III, 46   149 × 197 mm   5⅞ × 7¾ inches

The Nasmyth Tomb, Thos Duncan, A.R.A., and D.O.Hill, R.S.A.

III, 47   193 × 142 mm   7⅝ × 5⁹⁄₁₆ inches

McKenzie's Tomb, Greyfriars [*with D.O. Hill and another man*]

III, 48   191 × 140 mm   7 9/16 × 5 1/2 inches

Tomb [of John Byres, d. 1635], Greyfriars

III, 49   200 × 156 mm   7⅞ × 6⅛ inches

243

[*The*] *Nasmyth's Tomb, Greyfriars, Edinburgh*
with the Recorder [*as well as Hill and others*]

III, 50   204 × 152 mm   8 × 6 inches

John Knox's House [*center*], *Edinburgh*

[*High Street, on the Royal Mile, probably photographed in 1844*]

III, 51   141 × 194 mm   5⁵⁄₁₆ × 7⁵⁄₈ inches

246

The Scott Monument, Edinburgh [*completed in 1846*]

III, 52   153 × 208 mm   6⅟₁₆ × 8³⁄₁₆ inches

246

The Scott Monument, Edinburgh
[*with Edinburgh Castle in the left background*]

III, 53   204 × 147 mm   8 × 5$\frac{13}{16}$ inches

Edinburgh Castle
[*photographed about 1844; in the foreground are builders on the site of the Scott Monument;*
probably with its architect, George Meikle Kemp, in the top hat]

III, 54   142 × 197 mm   5⁹⁄₁₆ × 7¾ inches

———

Royal Institution, Edinburgh
[later taken over by the Royal Scottish Academy; the Castle in the background]

III, 55   206 × 147 mm   8⅛ × 5¹³⁄₁₆ inches

Leith Docks
[Leith is Edinburgh's port on the Firth of Forth, adjoining Newhaven]

III, 61   198 × 144 mm   7¹³⁄₁₆ × 5¹¹⁄₁₆ inches

[The Scott Monument during its erection]

III, 78   387 × 305 mm   15³⁄₁₆ × 12 inches

[*The Scott Monument, with the Scottish National Gallery in the background at right and Edinburgh Castle crowning the hill at left*]

III, 75   296 × 388 mm   11⅝ × 15¼ inches

SOME LADIES

The daughters of the families who lived, as Hill did when he was first married, in the New Town (Edinburgh's fashionable district of Georgian houses) were apt subjects for Hill and Adamson's calotypes, and there are several photographs of "the beautiful Misses Binny," as they were known (later Mrs. Marrable and Mrs. James Webster), daughters of Graham Binny, Writer to the Signet; Margaret and Ann McCandlish (later Mrs. Arkley and Mrs. Meichton); Justine Monro, daughter of Sheriff George Monro of Linlithgowshire; and so on. Agnes and Ellen Milne went to the smart New Town's Moray House Academy for Young Ladies, as did three of Hill's nieces, the daughters of his sister Mary Watson. The Milnes were the daughters of an Edinburgh architect, James Alexander Milne, who had retired to Northampton to be near his eldest daughter Margaret, wife of Sir Moses Philip Manfield, a shoe manufacturer.

Also in the New Town, close to Hill's old home at Moray Place, is Doune Terrace. At Number 6 lived John Harden's son Robert and his wife, and here the whole Harden family spent long periods. "Mrs Barker" (page 267) may therefore well be Mrs. Jane Barker, Harden's daughter, wife of Frederic Barker (though in Lord Cockburn's album, Hill has captioned this photograph "Miss Parker"). Frederic Barker later became second Bishop of Sydney and Metropolitan of Australia.

The most aristocratic woman here is surely Grizel Baillie (1822–91), sister of the tenth Earl of Haddington, seen on page 257 in a typical fashion-plate pose and looking exactly like the 1844 drawing of her by J. R. Swinton in the Scottish National Portrait Gallery. An earlier Grizel Baillie (1665–1746) had written a Household Book, 1692–1733, which was published in 1911, but the nineteenth-century one, like so many people in Scotland at the time, was more interested in religious matters. In December 1888 she became deaconess at Bowden Presbyterian Church, near the village of St. Boswells, the first woman to attain such a position in Scotland.

Miss Grizzel [Grizel] Baillie [1822–91]

II, 5   198 × 148 mm   7¹³⁄₁₆ × 5¹³⁄₁₆ inches

The Sisters—[The] Misses Binny

II, 7   206 × 158 mm   8 1/16 × 6 3/16 inches

[The] Misses Binny

II, 20   199 × 151 mm   7⅞ × 5¹⁵⁄₁₆ inches

Mrs James Webster [née Jane Binny]

II, 9   206 × 154 mm   8⅛ × 6⅟₁₆ inches

260

[The] Misses Binny and Miss [Justine] Monro

II, 15   204 × 150 mm   8 × 5⅞ inches

Miss Justine Monro [*later married to Mr Gallie, a merchant in Trinidad*]

II, 8   201 × 150 mm   7¹⁵⁄₁₆ × 5⅞ inches

The Gowan:
'We twa hae run about the Braes and pu-ed the Gowans fine' (Burns)
[Miss Margaret McCandlish, later Mrs Arkley, and her sister Ann, later Mrs Meichton]

II, 74   155 × 207 mm   6⅛ × 8 9/16 inches

The sleeping flowergatherers—Study—The Misses McCandlish [Margaret and Ann]

II, 75   151 × 205 mm   5$\frac{15}{16}$ × 8$\frac{1}{16}$ inches

Miss McCandlish, Edinburgh [later Mrs Rishton; presumably an elder sister of Margaret and Ann, pages 263 and 264]

II, 14   194 × 139 mm   7⅝ × 5½ inches

Miss Kemp [*sister of George Meikle Kemp*]

II, 19   190 × 137 mm   7½ × 5⁷⁄₁₆ inches

266

Mrs Barker [photographed June 28th, 1844;
possibly Jane Sophia Barker, the married daughter of John Harden, page 138]

II, 21   197 × 141 mm   7¾ × 5⁹⁄₁₆ inches

Agnes and Helen [Ellen] Mylne [Milne] of Northampton
[note the birdcage at left, one of Hill and Adamson's favorite "properties"]

II, 58   194 × 141 mm   7⅝ × 5⁹⁄₁₆ inches

A Study

[erroneously identified by some as Charlotte Hill—see page 221]

II, 62   203 × 148 mm   8 × 5¹³⁄₁₆ inches

CHILDREN

Coming from a large family, Hill had many nephews and nieces, and their children appear in several calotypes. Nieces Sophia and Patricia Morris (pages 227, 228) lived in Great Stuart Street, which ran into Moray Place, where Hill and his first wife set up housekeeping. Patricia became Mrs. Orr, and Sophia married Charles Finlay (1788–1872), a lawyer who was for a time clerk to Lord Justice Hope. Three of their five children were favourite sitters.

The Finlays were a legal family: their third child, Herbert, became a district judge, and John Hope Finlay (1839–1907; page 284), named after Lord Justice Hope, was a lawyer who became Keeper of the General Register of Sasines and Hornings (the Scottish land registry). He was also active in Conservative politics and the Presbyterian Church. His elder sister, Sophia (pages 272 and 274), lived to be one hundred (with another Sophia—daughter of the fourth child, Constance—as companion). Before she died, she provided invaluable help in identifying a number of sitters in the Hill/Adamson calotypes.

'The Three Sleepers—Sophia Finlay, Annie Farney and Brownie—
my stolen and lamented terrier pup'

II, 59   199 × 136 mm   7⅞ × 5⅜ inches

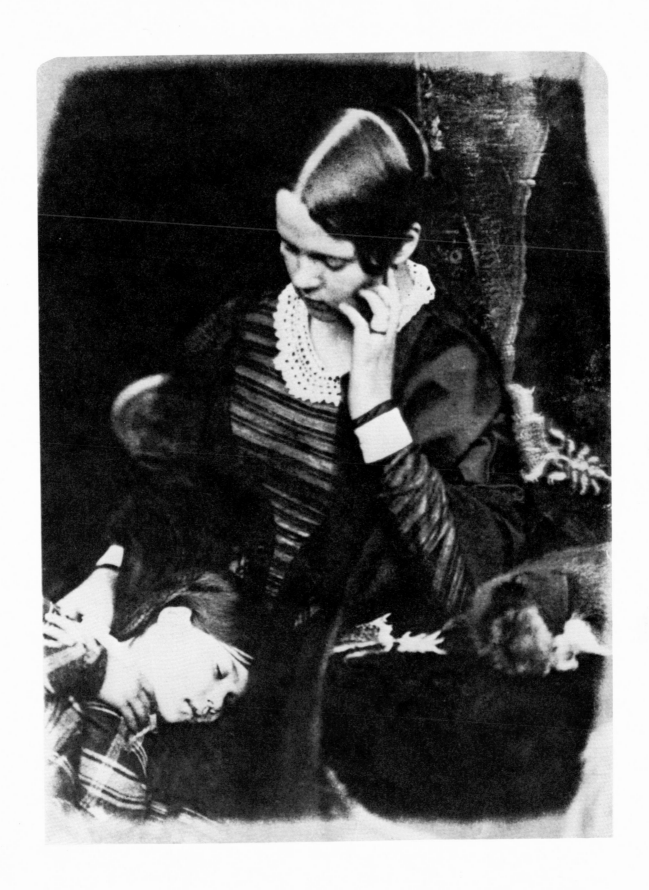

Asleep—[The] Misses Farney and Brownie

II, 60   208 × 155 mm   8³⁄₁₆ × 6⅛ inches

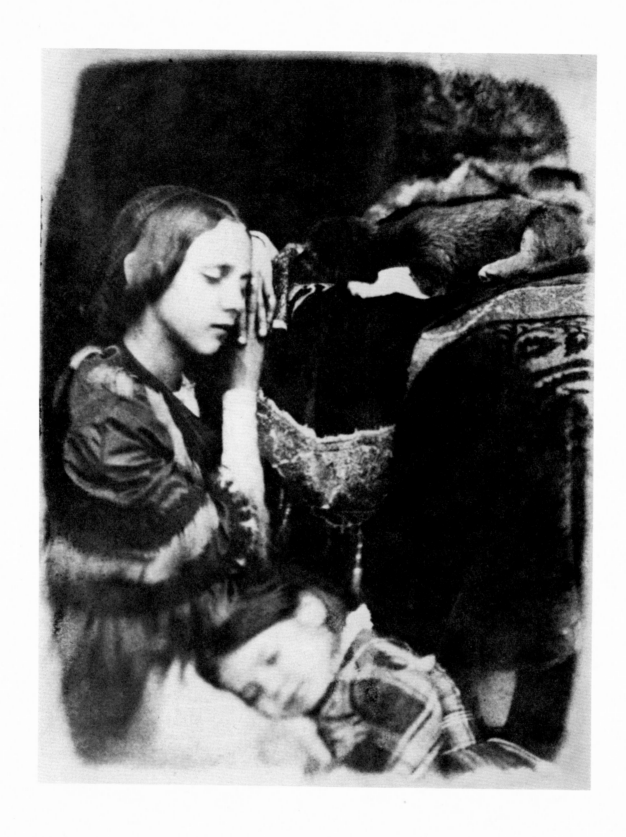

Sophie [Finlay], Annie [Farney] & Brownie—Sleep

II, 63   195 × 152 mm   7¹¹⁄₁₆ × 6 inches

274

Master [James] Miller [1837–68]

II, 64   200 × 142 mm   7⅞ × 5⁹⁄₁₆ inches

Master Miller

II, 65   195 × 136 mm   7¹¹⁄₁₆ × 5⅜ inches

[The] Misses Grierson

[daughters of the Reverend James Grierson, of Errol (?), photographed about 1845]

II, 66   194 × 141 mm   7⅝ × 5⁹⁄₁₆ inches

<hr>

[The] Misses Grierson

II, 71   200 × 145 mm   7⅞ × 5¾ inches

———————

Master Grierson [son of the Reverend James Grierson, of Errol (?)]

II, 77   189 × 138 mm   7⁷⁄₁₆ × 5⁷⁄₁₆ inches

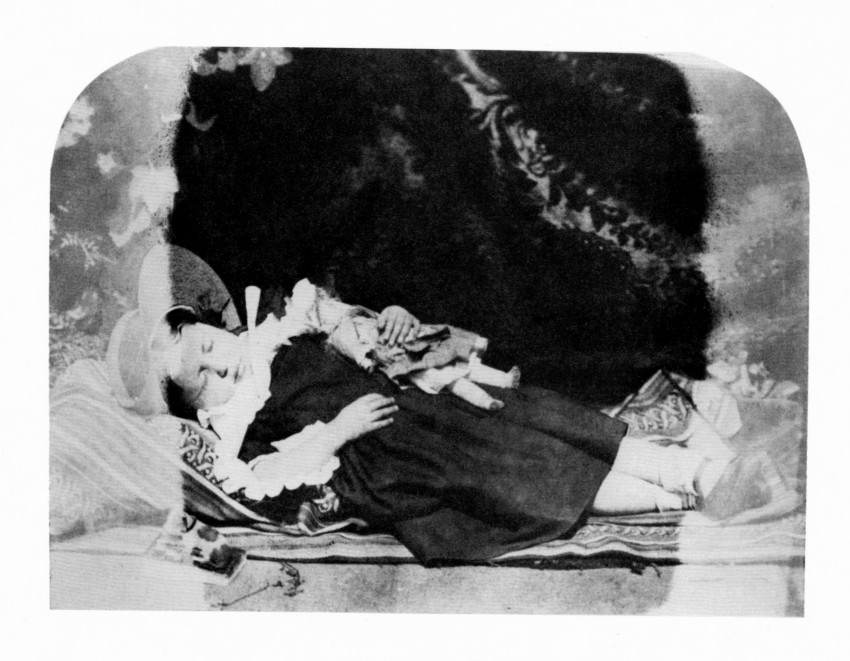

The Bedfellows—E. [Elizabeth] Logan
[1811–62, daughter of Sheriff H. J. Logan of Forfarshire]

II, 67   150 × 210 mm   5⅞ × 8¼ inches

A Sleeping Child—E. [Elizabeth] Logan

II, 70   150 × 206 mm   5⅞ × 8⅛ inches

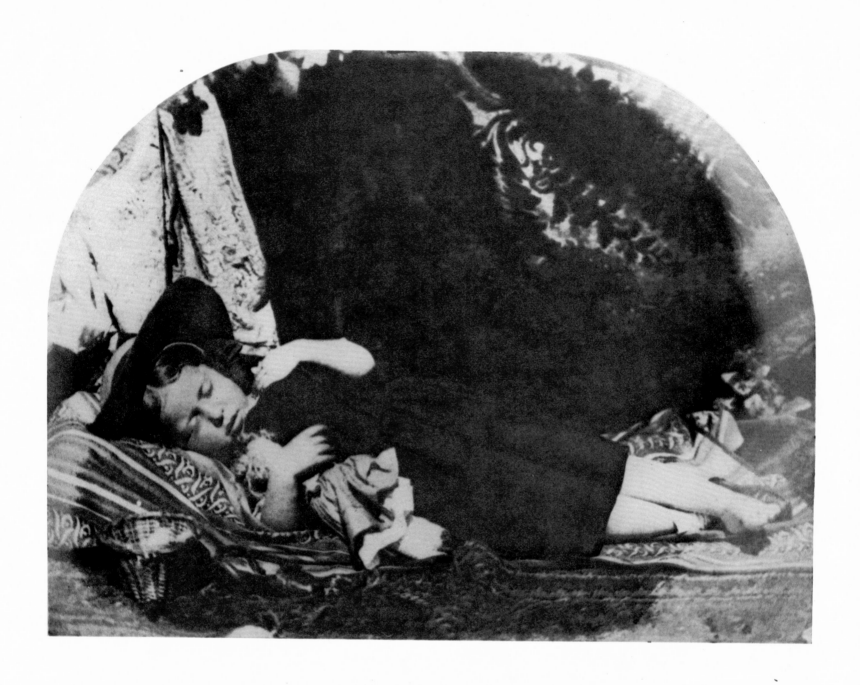

Elizabeth Logan

II, 76   156 × 212 mm   6⅛ × 8⁵⁄₁₆ inches

The Minnow Pool—Children of Mr Charles Finlay, Edinburgh

II, 69   209 × 157 mm   8¼ × 6³⁄₁₆ inches

Summer Noon—Master [John] Hope Finlay [1839–1907]

II, 72   150 × 209 mm   5⅞ × 8¼ inches

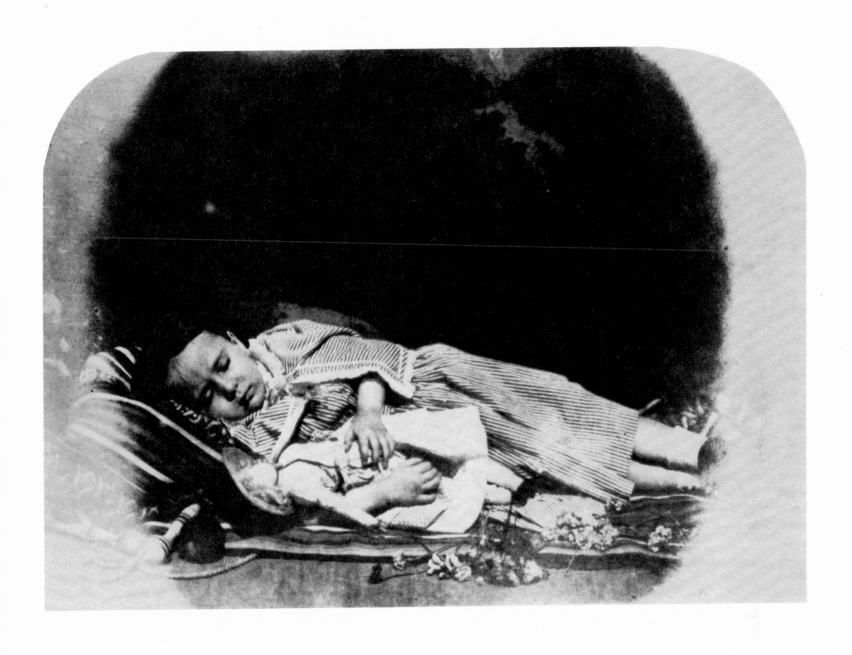

Sleeping Child—Miss Bell

II, 68   153 × 211 mm   6⅟₁₆ × 8⅝₁₆ inches

DRESSING UP

Hill and Adamson's genre pictures are perhaps the most overtly Victorian of their calotypes and the furthest removed from twentieth-century tastes. Many illustrate episodes in the works of Robert Burns and Sir Walter Scott, though whether Hill had any intention of turning his new medium of photography to his old profession of book illustration is not known.

The composition and posing of the portraits of the Reverend Peter Jones (pages 289, 290, 291) are of exactly the same nature as in the pictures of "Edie Ochiltree" (pages 301, 302, 303) and "The Monks of Kennaquhair" (page 292), but it is perhaps unfair to group them together under the heading "Dressing Up." Peter Jones was actually half American Indian and lived wholly as one until he was sixteen years old. "Kahkewaquonaby," his Indian name, can be translated as "Waving Plume." The names "Mr. Lane" and "Mr. Redding" (page 300) come from other prints of this photograph.

The blind Irish harpist Patrick Byrne (pages 293, 294, 295, 296) performed before Queen Victoria, and W. Leighton Leitch (pages 292, 297) was the Queen's drawing master for twenty-two years.

Ka[h]kewaquonaby, a Canadian Chief
[the Reverend Peter Jones, 1802–56, photographed between October 1844 and April 1846]

I, 83   191 × 140 mm   7⁹⁄₁₆ × 5½ inches

Ka[h]kewaquonaby—a Canadian Chief
[the Reverend Peter Jones]

I, 94   198 × 142 mm   7¹³⁄₁₆ × 5⁹⁄₁₆ inches

———

290

The Waving Plume (Canadian)
[Kahkewaquonaby, the Reverend Peter Jones]

II, 43 196 × 143 mm 7 11/16 × 5⅝ inches

———

291

[*W. Borthwick Johnstone, 1804–68, W. Leighton Leitch, 1804–83, and David Scott, 1806–64, as "The Monks of Kennaquhair"*]

II, 42   279 × 223 mm   11 × 8¹³⁄₁₆ inches

Irish Harper
[*Patrick Byrne, 1797 (?)–1863, a blind Irish harpist,*
perhaps to illustrate Scott's Lay of the Last Minstrel]

II, 44   204 × 154 mm   8 × 6¹⁄₁₆ inches

The Irish Harper's Hippocrene [*Patrick Byrne, photographed about 1843*]

II, 46   205 × 154 mm   8 1/16 × 6 1/16 inches

Irish Harper [*Patrick Byrne*]

II, 48   205 × 152 mm   8¼₁₆ × 6 inches

[Patrick] Byrne, the Irish Harper

II, 50   211 × 149 mm   8⁵⁄₁₆ × 5⁷⁄₈ inches

The House of Death [*W. Leighton Leitch, 1804–83*]

II, 45   193 × 142 mm   7⅝ × 5⁹⁄₁₆ inches

Mr Lane in an Indian Dress [*perhaps John Lane, actor*]

II, 47   191 × 145 mm   7⁹⁄₁₆ × 5¾ inches

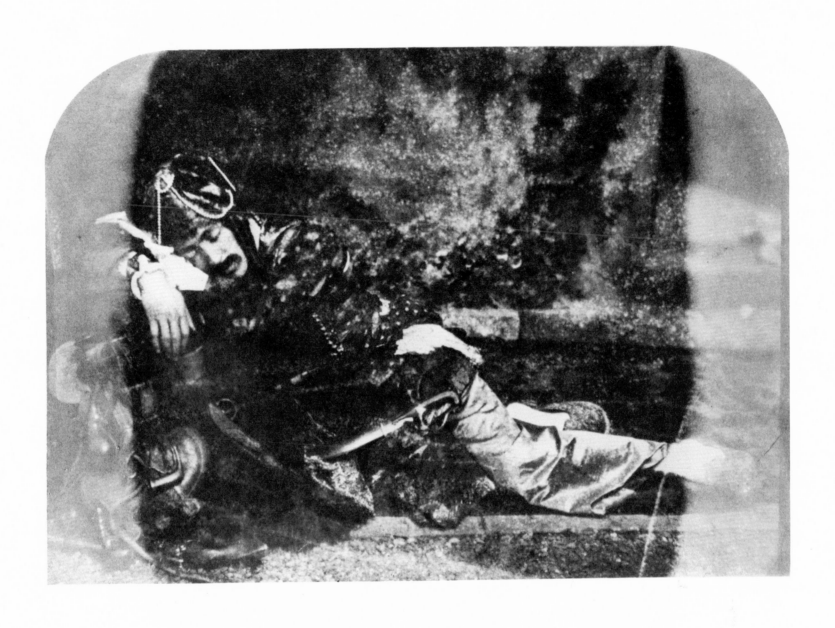

Mr Lane in an Indian Dress [*perhaps John Lane, actor*]

II, 55   142 × 204 mm   5⁹⁄₁₆ × 8 inches

_____

Afghan [African—that is, Moorish] Costume ["Mr Lane" and "Mr Redding"]

II, 57   194 × 140 mm   7⅞ × 5½ inches

Edie Ochiltree
[*John Henning, 1771–1851, as Ochiltree and Miss Cockburn as Miss Wardour,*
both characters from Scott's novel The Antiquary; *photographed at Bonaly, 1846 or 1847*]

II, 49   202 × 150 mm   7$\frac{15}{16}$ × 5$\frac{7}{8}$ inches

Edie Ochiltree (Henning) [*a character from Scott's* The Antiquary;
John Henning, photographed 1846 or 1847]

II, 54   204 × 153 mm   8 × 6 1/16 inches

Study in Bonaly—Edie Ochiltree (Henning) & Miss Wardour (Miss Cockburn)

II, 56   194 × 146 mm   7⅝ × 5¾ inches

BONALY AND
THE COUNTRYSIDE

Hill and Adamson took surprisingly few landscape photographs, and these few have little of the quality of their portraits. This was partly the nature of the calotype process, whose best results were obtained when the sensitized paper was exposed in the camera while still damp. Development had to start as soon as possible after exposure, and Adamson's high technical standards obviously demanded that the photographs be taken within easy access of his processing equipment, cumbersome to transport.

"Burnside, nr St Andrews" (page 306) is near the Adamson family home. The other five landscapes were taken on visits to Bonaly Tower, Colinton, home of Henry, Lord Cockburn, an Edinburgh lawyer who had close contacts with Hill. Both had been involved in the foundation of the Royal Scottish Academy and Cockburn was its legal adviser until he died in 1854. He gave Hill much encouragement in the Disruption painting project and often invited him, and all Edinburgh society, to his regular summer picnics. He and Lady Cockburn are seen at the foot of the stairs in the pictures on pages 308 and 309, which also show their three daughters as well as Henning and Hill.

Burnside, nr St Andrews, Fifeshire

III, 2   150 × 206 mm   5⅞ × 8⅛ inches

Colinton Manse [*and part of the old mill*]

III, 56   205 × 155 mm   8¹⁄₁₆ × 6⅛ inches

Bonaly, near Edinburgh—Lord Cockburn's residence

III, 57   147 × 202 mm   5¹³⁄₁₆ × 7¹⁵⁄₁₆ inches

[Bonaly, the residence of Lord Cockburn]

III, 58   153 × 207 mm   6¹⁄₁₆ × 8³⁄₁₆ inches

Trees at Bonaly

III, 59   190 × 149 mm   7½ × 5⅞ inches

A Tree—at Colinton

III, 60   203 × 148 mm   8 × 5¹³⁄₁₆ inches

ST. ANDREWS

St. Andrews, Fifeshire, is a fishing port and university town on the North Sea, about sixty miles northeast of Edinburgh, across the Firth of Forth. Because Sir David Brewster was Principal of the College of St. Salvator and St. Leonard in the university when his friend William Henry Fox Talbot wanted to promote his new invention of the calotype, St. Andrews played an important part in the history of photography in Britain. Some of the earliest calotypes ever made, those by Dr. John Adamson, Robert's elder brother, were taken there (see page 15). Both John and Robert often photographed its landmarks, its streets, and its scenery.

These eleven pictures from the National Portrait Gallery albums were presumably taken for Hill and Adamson's 1846 publication, *A Series of Calotype Views of St. Andrews Published by D. O. Hill and R. Adamson at their Calotype Studio, Calton Stairs, Edinburgh*, each copy of which had twenty-two positive calotypes pasted in.

The Argyle Gate, St Andrews

III, 62   193 × 137 mm   7⅞ × 5⁷⁄₁₆ inches

315

The Cathedral and Tower of St Regulus, St Andrews

III, 63   197 × 141 mm   7¾ × 5⁹⁄₁₆ inches

316

St Andrews [the Argyle Gate]

III, 64   186 × 145 mm   7⁵⁄₁₆ × 5¾ inches

317

St Mary's Chapel, St Andrews

III, 65   191 × 141 mm   7⁹⁄₁₆ × 5⁹⁄₁₆ inches

Cardinal Beaton Castle, St Andrews

III, 67   140 × 196 mm   5½ × 7¹¹⁄₁₆ inches

Fishmarket, St Andrews

III, 68   143 × 187 mm   5⅝ × 7⅜ inches

320

College Church, St Andrews

III, 69   188 × 137 mm   7⅞ × 5⁷⁄₁₆ inches

St Andrews Harbour

III, 70   140 × 197 mm   5½ × 7¾ inches

The Spindle Rock—near St Andrews

III, 71 142 × 196 mm 5⁹⁄₁₆ × 7¹¹⁄₁₆ inches

St Mary's Chapel, St Andrews

III, 72   130 × 192 mm   5⅛ × 7⁹⁄₁₆ inches

St Mary's Chapel, St Andrews

III, 73   189 × 146 mm   7⁷⁄₁₆ × 5¾ inches

SOME OTHER
PLACES

Only one of the pictures in this section—the first—was captioned by Hill. Those of Durham Cathedral were probably taken on the way to or from the York meeting of the British Association for the Advancement of Science in October 1844; certainly, Lady Eastlake saw a calotype of the cathedral in December of that year (see page 29). The photograph of Linlithgow Town Hall (pages 332–3) was probably taken in 1845, as the negative of another view, now in Glasgow University Library, is dated July 28th, 1845. These were studies for a painting of the town commissioned from Hill by John Miller, the railway engineer, of Leithen Lodge, Leithenhopes, Peebles.

The three large pictures were taken with Adamson's mammoth two-foot-square camera, which needed such long exposures that it was found to be quite unsuitable for portraits (though the picture "Two Fisherwomen," page 186, seems to have been taken with it). The two other calotypes taken with this camera in the National Portrait Gallery albums are both of the Scott Monument in Edinburgh (pages 251 and 252–3).

Linlithgow Palace [*probably photographed on July 28th, 1845*]

III, 66   147 × 199 mm   5¹³⁄₁₆ × 7⅞ inches

[Durham Cathedral, photographed in 1844]

III, 74   301 × 389 mm   11$\frac{13}{16}$ × 15$\frac{5}{16}$ inches

[Linlithgow Town Hall, with the town square fountain in the foreground, photographed in 1845]

III, 76   304 × 395 mm   12 × 15⁹⁄₁₆ inches

[*Durham Cathedral from across the River Wear, photographed in 1844*]

III, 77   304 × 392 mm   12 × 15⅞₆ inches

REVEREND AND
OTHER GENTLE FOLK

This section includes second poses of six men who appear in "The Disruption Painting" section of this book: Jabez Bunting (page 345), Thomas Chalmers (page 338), John Gibson (page 343), Alexander Keith (page 346),* Samuel Miller (page 347), and Robert Cunningham Graham Spiers (page 362).

Also in this section are those whose Disruption poses are not in the National Portrait Gallery albums—Henry Duncan (page 358), Thomas Guthrie (page 341), David Irving (page 356), and Thomas Miller (and family, page 361)—as well as a number of ministers who cannot be identified in the painting, though they may have been photographed with a view to inclusion: George Cook (page 339),† Graham Fyvie (page 362), Thomas Henshaw Jones (page 354), Finlay McAllister (page 355), John Robertson (page 353), R. Scott (pages 348, 359), Samuel Smith (page 352), and Andrew Sutherland (page 349).

Portraits of nine other men and two other ladies complete this section—and the albums.

---

* Keith had two sons who were Edinburgh surgeons and amateur photographers: George Skene Keith (1819–1910) took daguerreotypes of Palestine in 1844, and Thomas Keith (1827–95) took many calotypes of Edinburgh between 1854 and 1856.
† A calotype of Cook by Dr. John Adamson, Robert's elder brother, also exists.

The Revd Thomas Chalmers, D.D.

I, 5   163 × 118 mm   6⁷⁄₁₆ × 4⅝ inches

Dr Cooke [1772–1845] of St Andrews

[The Reverend George Cook, Professor of Moral Philosophy at St Andrews]

I, 13   185 × 134 mm   7⁵⁄₁₆ × 5¼ inches

[Henry Roberts, 3rd Baron Rossmore, 1792–1860, M.P. for Monaghan,
related to Wemyss family]

I, 21   204 × 148 mm   8 × 5¹³⁄₁₆ inches

[The] Revd Thomas Guthrie [1803–73], Free Church, Edinburgh,
Author of a Plan for the Ragged Schools

I, 29   201 × 146 mm   7$\frac{15}{16}$ × 5$\frac{3}{4}$ inches

*[The Reverend Thomas Scott of Peel, near Jedburgh—
not "Mr Welsh," as captioned by Hill]*

I, 40   191 × 150 mm   7⁹⁄₁₆ × 5⅝ inches

J [John] Gibson, Government Inspector of Schools in Scotland

I, 42   204 × 142 mm   8 × 5⁹⁄₁₆ inches

Sir Wyndham Anstruther
[*Sir Windham Carmichael Anstruther, 1793–1869, Bart.*]

I, 43   155 × 114 mm   6⅛ × 4½ inches

———

[The] Revd Dr [Jabez] Bunting

I, 46   210 × 144 mm   8¼ × 5¹¹⁄₁₆ inches

[The] Revd Dr [Alexander] Keith, Author of Several Works on Prophecy
[A duplicate of this calotype—numbered I, 30, and measuring 206 × 154 mm—
is also included in the National Portrait Gallery albums]

I, 48   203 × 152 mm   8 × 6 inches

———

[The] Revd Samuel Miller
[1810–81, D. D., of Monifieth and St Andrew's Church, Glasgow]

I, 49   196 × 144 mm   7¹¹⁄₁₆ × 5¹¹⁄₁₆ inches

347

[The] Revd Mr [R.] Scott [of Dalmeny—not "Mr W. Scott of Letham,"
as captioned by Hill]

I, 53   199 × 145 mm   7⅞ × 5¾ inches

*[The Reverend Dr Andrew Sutherland, d. 1867, A.M.,
minister at St Andrew's Church, Dunfermline, 1837–55]*

I, 59   196 × 150 mm   7$\frac{11}{16}$ × 5$\frac{7}{8}$ inches

[Dr David Laing, 1793–1878, LL.D.,
Professor of Antiquities at Edinburgh University, 1854–61, and friend of Sir Walter Scott]

I, 60   185 × 137 mm   7⁵⁄₁₆ × 5⁵⁄₁₆ inches

[*Hill's caption consists of a pencil line:*
he had obviously forgotten the sitter, who now is unidentifiable]

I, 63   204 × 150 mm   8 × 5⅞ inches

[The] Revd Mr [Samuel] Smith [1798–1868], Free Church, Borgue

I, 65   202 × 141 mm   7¹⁵⁄₁₆ × 5⁹⁄₁₆ inches

[The] Revd Mr [John] Robertson [1801–66], USC [United Scottish Church] Edin[burgh—also at Saline]

I, 67   203 × 146 mm   8 × 5¾ inches

[The] Revd Mr [Thomas Henshaw] Jones
[1796–1860, originally a member of the Church of England]

I, 73   207 × 153 mm   8³⁄₁₆ × 6¹⁄₁₆ inches

[The] Revd J [Finlay] McAllister [1805–66], Crieff

I, 75   197 × 142 mm   7¾ × 5⁹⁄₁₆ inches

Dr [David] Irving [1778–1860], Advocates' Library, Edin[burgh, present at the Disruption]

I, 77   201 × 138 mm   7$\frac{15}{16}$ × 5$\frac{7}{16}$ inches

Mr [Robert] Bryson [1778–1852], Edinburgh [horologer, and watchmaker to Queen Victoria;
his shop was at 66 Princes Street, almost next door to that of Alexander Hill, D. O. Hill's brother]
[A duplicate of this calotype—numbered I, 38 and measuring 208 × 149 mm—
is also included in the National Portrait Gallery albums]

I, 80   203 × 150 mm   8 × 5⅞ inches

[The] Revd Dr [Henry] Duncan of Ruthwell [1774–1846],
Propounder of Savings Banks &c.

I, 88   203 × 150 mm   8 × 5⅞ inches

[The] Revd Mr [R.] Scott

I, 89   198 × 140 mm   7$\frac{13}{16}$ × 5$\frac{1}{2}$ inches

[James Fillans, 1808–52, of Paisley and his two daughters—one is Wilhelmina;
Fillans was a sculptor, working in London from 1836 to 1852]

II, 18   203 × 163 mm   8 × 6⁷⁄₁₆ inches

[The] Rev. Thos [Thomas] Miller & Family,
Free Church Missionary in the Cape of Good Hope

II, 36   136 × 182 mm   5⅜ × 7⅛ inches

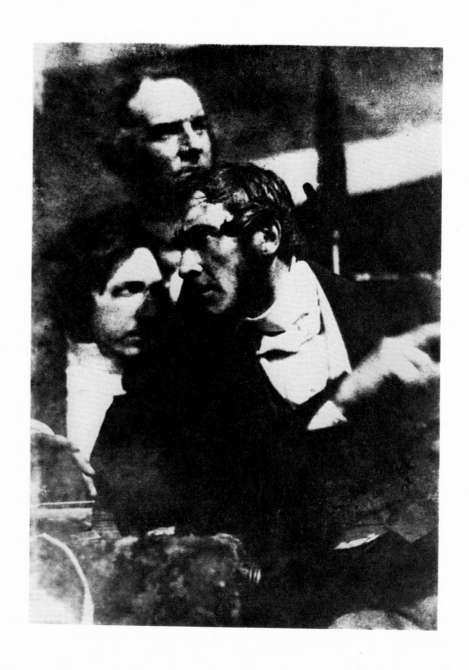

[The] Revd [Graham] Fyvie, Mr [Robert] Cadell, publisher,
Mr [Robert Cunningham Graham] Spiers [1797–1847, sheriff of Midlothian]

II, 37   155 × 113 mm   6⅛ × 4⁷⁄₁₆ inches

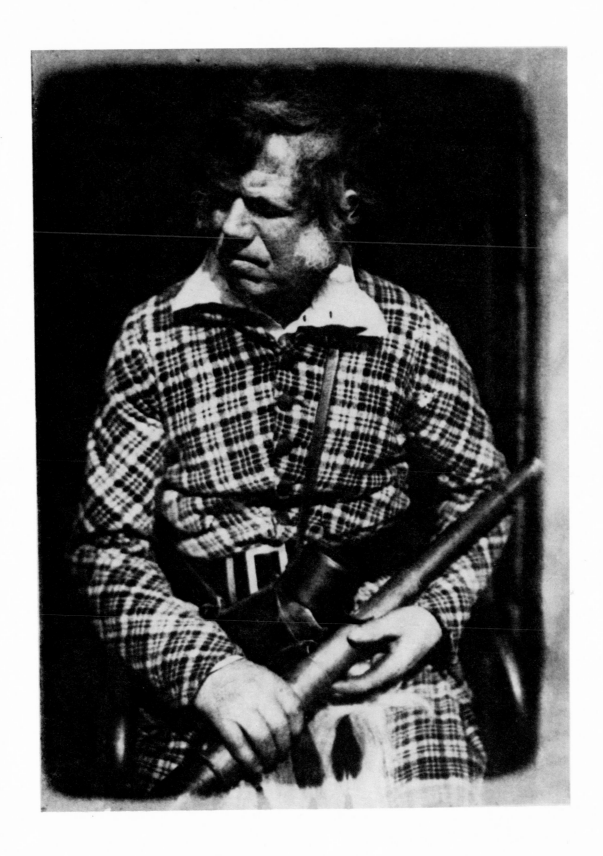

Finlay of Colonsay, a Deerstalker
[*to Campbell of Islay, photographed April 17th, 1846*]

I, 96   201 × 145 mm   7¹⁵/₁₆ × 5¾ inches

INDEX

References to figures and photographs appear
in **boldface type**.

A NOTE ABOUT

COLIN FORD AND ROY STRONG

————

Colin Ford joined the National Portrait Gallery, London, as its first Keeper of Film and Photography in 1972, having been Deputy Curator of Great Britain's National Film Archive for the previous seven years. He was Visiting Lecturer at California State University (Long Beach) from 1962 to 1964, during which time he also lectured for the University of California (Los Angeles). His study of the eminent British portrait photographer Julia Margaret Cameron, *The Cameron Collection*, was published in 1975.

Roy Strong is Director of the Victoria and Albert Museum and was formerly Director of the National Portrait Gallery. He has written extensively on the civilisation of Tudor and Stuart England. His many books include *Portraits of Queen Elizabeth I* (1963), *Holbein and Henry VIII* (1967), *The English Icon: Tudor and Jacobean Portraiture* (1967), *Splendour at Court: Renaissance Spectacle and the Theatre of Power* (1973), and, with Stephen Orgel, *Inigo Jones: The Theatre of the Stuart Court* (1973). In 1974 he delivered the Walls Lectures at the Pierpont Morgan Library. He has been closely associated in Britain with the promotion of exhibitions and scholarship in the field of photography. In 1968 he staged the first major retrospective ever held in a national collection of a living photographer, Cecil Beaton, and became the first chairman of the Arts Council's Photographic Exhibitions Committee.

A NOTE ABOUT

THE TYPE

———————

The text of this book was set in *Olympus*, a film version of
Trump Mediaeval. Designed by Professor Georg Trump in the
mid-1950's, Trump Mediaeval was cut and cast by the C. E.
Weber Typefoundry of Stuttgart, West Germany. The roman
letterforms are based on classical prototypes, but Professor
Trump has imbued them with his own unmistakable style.
The italic letterforms, unlike those of so many other typefaces,
are closely related to their roman counterparts. The result is
a truly contemporary type, notable both for
its legibility and versatility.

This book was composed by Superior Printing,
Champaign, Illinois; printed by Rapoport Printing Corp.,
New York, New York; and bound by American Book–Stratford
Press, Saddle Brook, New Jersey.
Design by Cynthia Krupat.